MARTIAL ARTS SERIES

Aikido
Techniques & Tactics

Gary Bennett

American Tejitsu Academy
10th-Dan Black Belt, Tejitsu Aikido
3rd-Dan Black Belt, Yoseikan Aikido

Human Kinetics

Library of Congress Cataloging-in-Publication Data

Bennett, Gary, 1953-
   Aikido techniques & tactics / Gary Bennett.
      p.   cm. -- (Martial arts series)
   Includes bibliographical references and index.
   ISBN 0-88011-598-X
   1. Aikido. I. Title.
  GV1114.35.B46   1997
  796.815'4--dc21   97-18748
                                                  CIP

ISBN: 0-88011-598-X

Acquisitions Editor: Kenneth Mange; **Developmental Editor:** Julie A. Marx; **Assistant Editor:** Jacqueline Eaton Blakley; **Editorial Assistant:** Jennifer Hemphill; **Copyeditor:** Allen Gooch; **Proofreader:** Erin Cler; **Indexer:** Theresa Schaefer; **Graphic Designer:** Robert Reuther; **Graphic Artist:** Tara Welsch; **Photo Editor:** Boyd LaFoon; **Cover Designer:** Jack Davis; **Cover Photograph:** Ray Malace; **Interior Photographs:** Gary Bennett; **Printer:** United Graphics

Human Kinetics books are available at special discounts for bulk purchase. Special editions or book excerpts can also be created to specification. For details, contact the Special Sales Manager at Human Kinetics.

Printed in the United States of America   10 9 8 7 6 5 4

Human Kinetics
Web site: www.humankinetics.com

United States: Human Kinetics, P.O. Box 5076, Champaign, IL 61825-5076
800-747-4457
e-mail: humank@hkusa.com

Canada: Human Kinetics, 475 Devonshire Road, Unit 100, Windsor, ON N8Y 2L5
800-465-7301 (in Canada only)
e-mail: orders@hkcanada.com

Europe: Human Kinetics, Units C2/C3 Wira Business Park, West Park Ring Road
Leeds LS16 6EB, United Kingdom
+44 (0) 113 278 1708
e-mail: hk@hkeurope.com

Australia: Human Kinetics, 57A Price Avenue, Lower Mitcham, South Australia 5062
08 8277 1555
e-mail: liahka@senet.com.au

New Zealand: Human Kinetics, P.O. Box 105-231, Auckland Central
09-523-3462
e-mail: hkp@ihug.co.nz

THIS BOOK IS DEDICATED TO DEBRA, WHO HAS BEEN MY CONSTANT INSPIRATION, AND TO MARTIAL-ARTS STUDENTS EVERYWHERE WHO ARE LOOKING FOR A WAY TO MAKE THE TRANSITION TO A TRUE STREET "DEFENSE" SYSTEM.

CONTENTS

PREFACE

To some, Aikido is a very spiritual study in the unification of mind, body, and spirit. To others, who seek the combat principles of its predecessor, Aiki-bujitsu, it is a true martial art in every sense of the word, with outstanding self-defense applications. The true nature of Aikido has been hotly disputed ever since O'Sensei's (Aikido's founder) "spiritual awakening" and his restructuring of the teaching principles of Hombu Aikido. Perhaps the answer to this debate lies somewhere between or in a combination of both aspects.

The purpose of this book is to illustrate and teach the street applicability of selected Aikido techniques. Although the combat drills and the self-defense applications illustrated here are derived from the Tejitsu system of Aikido, this book is not meant to detail only that system. Nor are the techniques presented in this book demonstrated exactly as they are performed in Tejitsu Aikido. Rather, the purpose here is to provide the reader with solid self-defense principles and show how they may be adapted specifically to Aikido techniques. With the incredible number of variations possible, and given the limited scope of this book, a comprehensive study of any Aikido system would be impossible. My intention, therefore, is to offer a detailed analysis of techniques that most Aikido systems have in common and present the highest-quality instruction in their use.

By gearing this text toward beginning and intermediate Aikido students and using the techniques with which they are familiar, I am able to reveal the hidden combat applications of Aikido techniques and help students attain a more comprehensive understanding of the roots and origins of their art. This book can also be a valuable resource to the advanced students of Aikido or to students from any other martial-art system who wish to delve into the practices of different systems and round out their education by learning some essential combat and grappling skills.

This book will allow students, no matter what their system or background, to learn and understand the effectiveness of Aikido applications through a painstakingly prepared combination of detailed text, abundant photo illustrations, tactical tips, and concise lists of dos and don'ts when practicing each technique. All of this is designed to help students learn the techniques presented without falling victim to common errors that reduce effectiveness, thus saving them much time and frustration in their practice. In short, I have designed this text not to present an overview of the topic but rather to provide students with all the tools necessary to actually learn the techniques.

Chapters 1 through 4 will familiarize the reader with some background and history of Aikido and with basic Aiki principles such as nonresistance and the circular nature of Aikido techniques. The reader will also be instructed in the use of defensive parries and counterstriking methods necessary for close-quarter self-defense, and in the concept of justifiable force. Chapters 5 through 11 will detail the application of specific techniques against punching attacks; grabs; combination-attack sequences commonly used in the harder styles such as Karate, Taekwondo, and Tang Soo Do; and weapon attacks. Chapter 12 will address general fitness tips.

The benefits of studying Aikido are many and can be different to each student. The practice will help some attain a spiritual balance by fostering inner peace and tranquillity through development of the spirit. Others will find that the practice of Aikido helps them develop a fuller life through attaining new levels of self-worth, confidence, and self-discipline. Still others may dwell entirely on the achievement of increased physical stamina, strength, flexibility, and the ability to defend oneself and one's family. Aikido does not mold the student into something new but allows the student to find and enhance his or her own path and interests.

ACKNOWLEDGMENTS

I would like to express my deepest appreciation to my former instructors for their patience in, and devotion to, the teaching of the martial arts, especially those instructors who understood and nurtured my hunger for new material and my quest to find the hidden combat applications within the arts that they taught me.

A special thanks goes out to Soke Daniel Stanton, ninth dan of the New World Martial Arts Association, who was the first to officially recognize my system.

I will always be grateful to Shihan John Kanzler of the Eastern USA International Martial Arts Association, who has helped me immeasurably along the way and who has become my dear friend.

I am also grateful to the membership committee of the World Head of Family Sokeship Council for granting me admission not only to its outstanding and prestigious organization but also to its Hall of Fame. To be ranked among the men and women of this organization is to be recognized as one of the "best of the best." I hope I can continue to live up to the high ideals and standards of these fine men and women.

My sincere thanks go to the students and instructors of the Tejitsu Aikido Hombu Dojo for their help in performing the techniques shown here. Thanks also to Sensei David Bednarczyk, who took a real beating as my partner in my video series, and to Sensei Eugene Driscoll for his instruction in sword and knife fighting.

Finally, my thanks goes to Michael Soohey for his friendship and his coverage of my system; he is responsible for the exposure I have received in numerous martial-arts magazines and video documentaries.

CHAPTER

GETTING

STARTED

ikido is a Japanese martial-art system designed to teach a nonaggressive approach to combat based on joint locks and throws that were derived from ancient forms of Jujitsu. Aikido stresses nonresistance, redirection of force, and blending with the force of the attacker. It is a "Do," or way-of-life, study, rather than strictly a combat system, in its traditional form. As such, many students achieve inner peace, harmony, and spiritual perfection.

Many branch systems of Aikido, as you will read later on, stress self-defense and the more combat-related roots of this art. Even though these systems do not emphasize the spiritual side of Aikido, all forms of Aikido stress the harmonious approach to combat as well as its practical influence on life in general. The harmony in technical applications merely means to blend with the attack of an aggressor rather than meet it head-on and fight force with force. Aikido is, after all, a "soft" martial system.

Before we get into the how-to of Aikido, we should explore some of the background of its philosophy, discipline, and values. We should also discuss some of the things that make Aikido, as an art and in training, different from other martial arts and discuss some of the benefits you may derive from Aikido training. Some of these will be similar to benefits derived from other systems; others will be unique to the study of Aikido.

The reasons each of us takes up martial-arts training are as varied as each individual. This chapter will discuss some of the reasons you may want to study the martial arts, which may help you decide which art to pursue. To help simplify the selection process, I have provided information on seeking instruction; choosing instructors, schools, locations, and pricing plans; and selecting a preferable class size for the beginner.

THE VALUE OF AIKIDO

Aikido is something different to each of us, and the benefits each of us derives from its practice are extremely varied. Aikido is unique among the martial arts in that a student gets out of it what he or she puts into it. Aikido does not forge a beginning student into a disciplined fighting machine, but rather presents a physical and spiritual means for each student to attain his or her own goals, whatever they may be.

The path to spiritual harmony and enlightenment is open to anyone who seeks to focus his or her energies along these lines. Those seeking increased levels of self-confidence, self-worth, and discipline are at home in Aikido as well. All who practice this form can achieve increased endurance, coordination, flexibility, and physical-fitness levels. Last, but certainly not least, the student learns essential self-defense aimed at also preserving the life of the attacker.

A most certain change in your mental state comes with this type of training. Unlike more aggressive arts, which help develop confidence but can also encourage arrogance of power, Aikido helps you develop a natural peace of mind from knowing that you are capable of defending yourself and your loved ones without the use of deadly force.

SEEKING INSTRUCTION

Once you have decided to study a martial art, your next steps are to decide which art you want to study and find a reputable school and instructor. The following sections will help you through this process with basic information about the characteristics of Aikido and how it is similar to and different from other martial arts, as well as what to look for in a school and instructor.

When I started seeking out instruction, I felt, as everyone does, the hesitation and even fear that can present themselves when walking into a strange dojo (school) to inquire about the system and training provided. This is perfectly natural. With what we have all seen on television and in the movies about martial arts, it is only natural to feel intimidated asking questions of the instructor. Instructors are nothing more than ordinary men and women with a specialized skill to offer the prospective student. Teachers have the student's best interests at heart and are only there to help.

WHICH ART DO I STUDY?

Which art to study is an extremely personal decision. It depends on many variables, including personality type, physical condition, and goals, to name a few. There are as many different types of martial arts as there are reasons for studying. Each individual must go through the selection process carefully to determine exactly which type he or she is really seeking.

More aggressive men and women may look to the harder styles such as Karate, Taekwondo, and Tang Soo Do. These martial arts emphasize punching and kicking focused on both attack and defense with contact between students during sparring sessions. Many people enjoy the physical contact, sparring, and development of physical power.

The striking and kicking techniques taught, though it is rarely specifically stated, are designed to be potentially lethal. The training does, of course, teach restraint on the part of the student to avoid confrontation at all cost. This does not change the fact that these techniques can easily kill. Hard styles generally rely heavily on high kicks to the upper body and head and require a much greater range of flexibility than does Aikido. Also, because these arts focus on overcoming force with force, they advocate more strength training and conditioning of the body to withstand the pain of repeated impacts.

More easygoing types may look to the "softer" arts for their training. Arts like Aikido, Judo, and Gung-fu (Kung-fu) are geared more toward passive self-defense and stress the nonaggressive point of view to their training. Although the term "nonaggressive martial art" may seem to be an oxymoron, it is not. What must be examined is the "intent" of the art. Proponents of hard styles think that the best defense is a good offense. Soft arts prefer to not initiate aggressive action of any kind. Although students of these arts may contend with another to defend themselves or someone else, there is no violent intent.

This is not to say that all people studying a particular art share the same characteristics. Many people are attracted by the system that is diametric to their personality type. Aggressive types may want a training system and philosophy that have a tendency to balance their lives, and the quieter types may seek to come out of their shells by taking a more violent art form. What is most important is that the system teaches good practical self-defense, balanced with a philosophy of respect and tolerance for others, and instruction in the use of *justifiable and legal force.*

Aikido training provides physical conditioning more along the lines of aerobic training with increased coordination, balance, endurance, and self-discipline. Since Aikido focuses on redirection of the attacker, much more attention is devoted to balance and coordination than to physical strength. The truth is that great muscle strength puts the Aikido practitioner at a disadvantage when learning the techniques. Aikido techniques are designed to be most effective when applied with minimum force. Those with less strength learn quickly to apply the techniques properly while those with great upper-body strength must go through an "unlearning" process to turn off the power that they have worked so long to attain.

Because of its nature, Aikido is well suited for persons of smaller stature, less physical strength, and less flexibility. It is an excellent training vehicle for women and smaller men. Although it does not require much physical strength, it will help to develop and tone what the student already has. Aikido students tend to develop viselike grips because their hands and forearms are constantly being used in the grips and locks. The great advantage of training in Aikido is that just about anyone can do it and be highly successful in applying what they have learned in a self-defense situation.

Along with these advantages, Aikido, by its noncombative nature, develops an attitude of true self-defense. Defensive action is taken without malice toward those who would do harm. The philosophy teaches the student to have the ability to do combat without the intent to harm the attacker. Each technique is specifically designed to disable the attacker with the minimum amount of force and damage.

CHOOSING AN INSTRUCTOR

If you have decided to study Aikido, your next question will most likely be: "How do I choose an instructor?" Good question. Should you look for rank, reputation, teaching philosophy, and personality? *Yes!* All these things are important.

Of course, you want to find the highest-ranked instructor possible. The higher the instructor's rank, generally the more instruction time and experience that person has accumulated. Some of you may have heard the popular "rule of thumb" that says never trust anyone who claims high rank. It is true that there are some fakers in all styles and systems; but by ruling out, for example, anyone over a sixth-degree black belt, you could be missing the best instruction possible. Take a middle path; instead of immediately ruling out instructors of a certain rank, evaluate those with both high and low ranks equally.

The reputation of an instructor is of utmost importance because it reflects the attitude of the person. Get several opinions of an instructor's reputation, preferably from current and past students. Don't make a decision based solely on the advice of a competing school or instructor. Any instructor who disparages another is *not* the one to choose.

Teaching philosophy and personality are inseparable. An overly aggressive or abusive instructor is exactly that type of individual. Look for an instructor who is calm and respectful in dealing with students. Teacher and student must have mutual respect for each other. If the teacher demands high respect from the students, yet does not respect them in return, then students will not find a supportive environment in which to learn Aikido.

Find out who will actually be teaching the classes. Many times a school will be under the supervision of a prominent, high-ranking master instructor, but all the teaching is left to the higher-ranking students in the class. It is always desirable to train with no less than a second-degree black-belt instructor. My best advice is to watch classes, get information, check rankings, and watch some more classes. If an instructor will not permit you to view a class in progress, you know that you can safely rule that one out!

CHOOSING A SCHOOL

Factors other than the instructor are also important when choosing a school. The overall package, including location, facilities, class size, and pricing plans, must be weighed when making your decision.

Location. A prominent location and high-priced rental property can indicate a successful school; after all, location is the number one factor in determining the success of any business, and it can predict whether or not the school will be around next year. But one of the most important considerations is whether the school is in a safe neighborhood. Don't put yourself in harm's way to get to a self-defense class!

In addition, you might consider choosing a qualified instructor and school close to your home or your place of work to make it easier for you to attend class. The easier it is for you to reach your class, the more likely you will be motivated to attend!

Facilities. The physical layout of the school itself should have little effect on the quality of instruction. Some of the greatest instructors have taught students in their yards, driveways, dining rooms, and other extremely modest accommodations. However, if you prefer multiple training rooms, new equipment, shower facilities, and other amenities, be sure to include these in your list of qualities when searching for a school.

When visiting the school, the most important thing to consider should be the cleanliness of the dojo itself. No matter how extravagant or modest, the dojo must be clean, well cared for, and orderly. The state of the dojo in many ways can reflect the instructor's teaching philosophy. A dirty, cluttered dojo not only is hazardous but also could indicate a school with financial problems or a general lack of concern for the students.

Class Size. The size of the class is a highly individual matter. Some people enjoy the relative anonymity of being in a large group, while others prefer to get the more individualized attention of a small group. Those who can afford it and tend to be very self-conscious may even opt for private lessons.

Generally speaking, you should avoid a class of more than 20 students because the instructor will be spread too thin to give proper attention to everyone. It is always a good idea to have a mix of men and women of varying ages and abilities in each class. Because all of us are different in strength and ability, we become teachers to the people with whom we are training. The most important thing to remember is that everyone goes through the beginner stage of not wanting to look clumsy, awkward, or foolish in front of other people. This fear is perfectly normal, and we have all been through it, including the instructor. That person was a beginner at some point, too, and well understands how you are feeling.

Pricing Plans. Prices for instruction can vary greatly, ranging from $20 a month on up; prices average between $40 and $55 a month. Most schools have a dues system in which students pay up front each month for that month's training; others require the signing of a contract and payment up front for a specific time, usually six months to a year. Still others charge membership fees for the contract period and force students to "rejoin" and pay the membership fee on top of class dues with every contract extension. It is wise to beware of any business that requires an extended payment in advance. Many a health-club member has wound up holding a worthless membership card and contract receipt after the club closed.

Schools that have contracts will generally include the cost of your gi (uniform) in that contract price. Those that charge by the month sometimes include uniforms when running specials to attract new students. Others will charge you for them separately after you are sure you want to stay. The average retail cost is $30. Cost of belts can either be separate or be included in the school's testing fees. The individual retail cost for belts is about $5. Testing fees vary by the level for which you are testing and can run from

$10 to $25 for lower ranks and $50 to several hundred dollars for black-belt degrees.

AIKIDO BELTS

Belt ranking in Aikido is divided into two classes, kyu ranks (below black belt) and dan ranks (black belt). The following are generalized rank requirements extrapolated from several Aikido systems. These ranking periods and requirements to advance vary from system to system, but the following information should provide a broad idea of how rank is attained.

KYU RANKS

Kyu ranks are awarded strictly on the basis of technical proficiency and mastery of the material presented within each rank. Throughout the kyu ranks, the students wear the traditional white gi. In many styles, but not all, students at brown-belt level are considered to be advanced students and may wear either the white jacket with black trousers or simply the hakama with a white jacket. The hakama is an ankle-length pleated skirt that was worn by the ancient samurai. Its purpose was to conceal the movement of the feet. Many instructors consider this to be counterproductive when trying to teach students proper footwork.

Originally the only belt colors were white and black. The ranks in between had no outward designation. Some schools still hold to this, while others use a colored-belt ranking system such as the one shown in table 1.1. Even within the colored-belt systems, there is a great deal of diversity. There is as much diversity in the requirements for obtaining rank as there are different Aikido systems. Table 1.1 also illustrates the differences in the required training time for each rank for four systems of Aikido.

Most systems have a specific "time in grade" requirement or prescribed time frame between each level. Promotions are primarily based on achieving a certain level of technical proficiency in the material presented. Other schools may also require some sort of successful "free form" defense against multiple attackers as part of their testing.

TABLE 1.1
A Typical Belt-Ranking System in Three Aikido Styles

Rank	Name	Belt	Hombu	Yoseikan	Tejitsu
6th kyu	Rokyu	White	Beginner	Beginner	Beginner
5th kyu	Gokyu	Orange	40 hours*	36 hours	24 hours
4th kyu	Yonkyu	Green	40 hours	36 hours	24 hours
3rd kyu	Sankyu	Blue	30 hours	72 hours	48 hours
2nd kyu	Nikyu	Brown	60 hours	72 hours	48 hours
1st kyu	Ikkyu	Brown	60 hours	72 hours	48 hours

*Each rank's time in hours represents the minimum additional hours of training required after achieving the previous rank.

DAN RANKS

Dan ranks are awarded in three ways. The first is through mastery of additional technical material, the second is through accumulation of additional teaching time, and the third is through what is called "honorary" or "service" promotion. This third type is for service to the promotion and betterment of the art and primarily applies to ranks over third dan. This promotion could be achieved, for example, by pulling up roots and taking the art to another country. It requires a higher commitment to the art than to yourself.

Any given martial art generally has 10 black-belt rankings. The highest dan ranking attainable varies among different Aikido systems, as do the specific requirements for each level. Very little information has been published or is available regarding advanced dan rankings of most systems. Table 1.2 contains the Japanese terms and most common titles of the 10 dan ranks.

Although the attainment of a black belt may seem to the beginner to be the ultimate goal or achievement, there is only one correct answer to what it means to be a black belt. It means beginner, period! Reaching the level of black belt means that you have finally reached a level within the art in which you can begin to really understand what it is all about. It is a realization of how much there is left to learn and should be a humbling experience.

TABLE 1.2 Black-Belt Ranks			
Title*	**Rank**	**Name**	**Belt Worn**
Hanshi or Grandmaster	10th dan	Judan	Red
Kyoshi, Shihan, or Master	9th dan	Kudan	Red and Black or Red and White
Kyoshi, Shihan, or Master	8th dan	Hachidan	Red and Black or Red and White
Kyoshi, Shihan, or Master	7th dan	Shichidan	Red and Black or Red and White
Kyoshi, Shihan, or Master	6th dan	Rokudan	Red and Black or Red and White
Kyoshi, Shihan, or Master	5th dan	Godan	Red and Black or Red and White
Kyoshi, Shihan, or Master	4th dan	Yondan	Red and Black or Red and White
Renshi or Sensei	3rd dan	Sandan	Black
Renshi or Sensei	2nd dan	Nidan	Black
Renshi or Sensei	1st dan	Shodan	Black

* Titles used and color of belts worn vary among different systems.

To hold a black belt means that a person has a certain amount of respect due him or her from the other students as an instructor in training. It also carries a responsibility toward the lower students; the black-belt holder is elevated above the peer level to a parental role in which the student's benefit is more important than his or her own. Black belts are required to have a higher level of commitment than the average student and set the proper examples in attitude and intent.

Many martial-art systems (thankfully this is rare in Aikido) have a practice of giving black belts to children; I highly disagree with this practice. A child may be technically proficient but cannot possibly have the maturity to take on the moral, philosophical, and parental responsibilities of being a teacher. The child has not had enough life experience to handle his or her own emotions and problems, let alone help others with theirs.

I hope the information presented in this chapter will be helpful to you in making some crucial decisions regarding your journey in Aikido. No matter what path you choose or what your goals are, remember that none is right or wrong. Each person must decide which road to travel. As with all aspects of life, do the research and choose wisely what is best for you. The material in the next chapter will give you some fascinating background information on the martial arts in general and on the development of Aikido.

CHAPTER

2

ROOTS
OF AIKIDO

Opinions differ about the origins of all the Japanese martial
arts because very few records were kept prior to Japan's
feudal era. Most histories that people hold dear are passed
down orally from teachers to students over many generations.
Even today, most of the legends surrounding martial arts history
still proliferate in this manner. I have tried to provide the most
accurate background information possible, derived from records
kept by those closest to the system originators, and avoid myths
and hearsay. The following represents the most popular theories
about the roots of martial arts in general and of Aikido in
particular.

THE HISTORY OF MARTIAL ARTS

The martial arts have been around as long as people themselves.
From the first time a human raised a hand or took up a stick or a

rock to attack a neighbor, formal combat training has been in existence. One of the earliest references to professional warriors is found in the Bible in Genesis 14:14, where Abram gathered together and armed his "trained servants" to go to war.

The martial arts actually traveled eastward from the Middle East to Asia, not vice versa as is commonly thought. As the human population grew, people inhabited more areas of the world, which brought about the spread of knowledge. Combat training came about from a need for specialized study in order to survive and was constantly adapted by each culture to the circumstances encountered. The ancient Greeks, Persians, Spartans, and Romans had no Asian masters to teach them the secrets of combat. Likewise, combat arts such as English boxing, French savate, and Russian sambo were developed from the European pool of knowledge, not from that of the Far East. The martial arts of Asia developed according to their own survival needs.

The Chinese record the development of their earliest martial art at about 2000 B.C. This system of training was called Wu Shu and is still popular today. The systems in China that we have heard about most often are called Gung-fu (Kung-fu), or Chinese boxing, which were introduced at the Siu Lum (pronounced "shao lin" in Mandarin) monastery in A.D. 520 by an Indian priest named Tamo or Bodhidharma. He introduced a system called the Eighteen Hands of Lo-han, which was the forerunner to the Five Formed Fist of Siu Lum (Shao Lin) Kung-fu.

Korea's oldest martial-art system, Hwarang-do, came into prominence in the mid–seventh century under the rule of Queen Songdok of the Silla kingdom, who sponsored a military-religious school for the children of the elite or noble class. King Chinhung later expanded this training into a philosophical life structure that predates Japan's Code of Bushido (see page 16).

The earliest recorded martial-arts event in Japan was a sumo match in the year 22 B.C. before Emperor Suinin, the 11th emperor of Japan. During the following centuries, the wrestling and harder forms of sumo made a split with Jujitsu, which was coming into existence as a system of its own. Just as today, the leading proponents of Jujitsu, primarily the samurai, had their own ideas and areas of specialization, resulting in many different systems.

Jujitsu was for centuries a generic name for many systems of bare-handed combat, with some of the first references dating back to the Heian period (A.D. 784-1184). Most of the empty-handed combat forms of the time were techniques that were incorporated into weapons systems and served as backup techniques for samurai who became disarmed in combat. It was not until the early part of the 16th century that these techniques were broken out, expanded, and organized into complete systems of bare-handed combat.

Aesthetic Jujitsu began to formally develop during the Edo period about A.D. 1600 and is generally considered to have been formally created in 1638 during the Tokugawa period by Ch'en Yuan-pin, an immigrant from China. Jujitsu's full emergence as a weaponless martial-art system hit its pinnacle during the Meiji and Taisho eras (1868-1926) and became, in part, the basis for Aikido.

THE DEVELOPMENT OF AIKIDO

About A.D. 1100, samurai general Shinra Saburo Yoshimitsu of the Minamoto family introduced an organized fighting and exercise program for the officers of his army that was at some point called Daito-ryu-aiki-jujutsu. This system was so effective that it was kept a family secret for centuries until it was taken over by the Takeda family of the Aizu clan. A great deal of confusion exists as to this point. According to Yamada and Macintosh (1966), Yoshimitsu named the system himself. However, Shioda (1968) reports that others believe that this system was originally created by Prince Teijun in the mid–19th century and was named Aikijutsu.

In either case, it is known that in 1910, Dr. Sogaku Takeda began to teach his successor, Professor Morihei Uyeshiba, the secrets of this ancient art. Professor Uyeshiba had already studied martial arts for 12 years, earning teaching certificates in both the Yagyu-shin-kage-ryu and Tenjin-shinyo systems of Jujitsu. During this time he also studied Kito-ryu Jujitsu and Yagi-ryu Kenjutsu. In 1918 he received a master's teaching certificate in Daito-ryu.

THE CODE OF BUSHIDO AND TODAY'S MARTIAL ARTS

The quintessential study of Bushido (military knight ways) was written by Inazo Nitobe and published in 1899. The following section is drawn from notes on Nitobe's work, information obtained from my instructors, and the teachings I received about British morality and chivalry.

The Bushi, or Fighting Knights as the samurai were otherwise known, were warriors with a rank of nobility much like the knights of Europe. As knights, they were granted higher status and, with such, were expected to behave with a higher moral and ethical standard than was the rest of the populace.

The knights of Europe and the samurai of Japan had a common background that is seldom taught today. Both groups were men-at-arms, professional warriors in service to a feudal lord. Their rank was bestowed upon them either by birth into a noble family or by meritorious service to the lord, country, or common good. In both Japanese and European cultures, these men lived and died by a code of honor, gallantry, generosity, and courtesy—in other words, chivalry. This is the lineage that we as martial artists all share. It is the tradition we must uphold.

It is no surprise if this does not sound like any martial artist or instructor you know because few teach the ancient code of Bushido. Unfortunately, what is being taught today in many of the arts is merely the art of war without the responsibility, culture, and ethics. We hear and read many stories of the great samurai battles and how many opponents were killed by a certain legendary fighter, but we never hear of the great warriors who were so averse to killing that they never tarnished their fine blades with the blood of another human being.

It is unfortunate that Americans first learned martial arts in Japan during a time filled with post–World War II hatred toward the occupying forces of the United States. It was the first time the former noble class of samurai descent had to teach their skills on a commercial basis to survive. Many of these proud people lost everything in the war and could not survive in the post-war world due to their naiveté regarding the ways of the business world, where honesty and integrity were not as important as they had been to the samurai. It is no wonder that the true meaning of Bushido was lost among many of those who brought it to other countries.

We as martial artists have a heritage that we share. We, by association with a given Japanese system, become a part of the family that extends back past the founder of a particular style to the ancient samurai clans of Japan. We must look deeper than the attitudes of those around us and those who teach violence and confrontation to the roots of our family trees, to the way of Bushido, the way it is supposed to be taught. We have an obligation, as part of our joint noble heritage, to uphold a higher standard of conduct and ethics.

This ceremonial Japanese warrior helmet is called a Kabuto.

VALUES OF THE SAMURAI

Believe it or not, Westerners share many values with the samurai clans of Japan. The following section correlates the European values of chivalry and morality with those of the East. Though different in many details of daily lifestyle, people are people in the West and the East.

• **Integrity**—Moral integrity was very much a part of the samurai way of life. Samurai were taught, and were expected at all times, to behave correctly and to live and die, if necessary, for what was right or just. Samurai would no more take part in underhanded or dishonest dealings than they would sell their families into slavery. This precept was the cornerstone upon which all decisions of life were made. The term *gishi*, or man of integrity, was the highest title that could be given. It was more cherished a title than any other. To act in a manner that was unbecoming or dishonest would be the ultimate sin, bringing shame upon the family and its name.

- **Valor**—Personal bravery or the strength of purpose and resolve that enables one to stand fast in the face of danger goes hand in hand with the samurai sense of justice. Courage was all important to the samurai. The willingness to stand and die for the sake of righteousness was the mark of their birth. To complain about physical hardship or the need to endure hardships was the mark of a coward. Discipline was a big part of training the young. They were taught to endure hardships, hunger, and cold and to confront their worst fears so they might be able to stand when tested for what was right and just.

This teaching included not just bravery in the face of the enemy, but the bravery to face all that life had to offer as well, much like the trials and tribulations with which we are all tested. To shirk one's duty to family and to fail to meet one's obligations were as much cowardice as running away during battle.

- **Compassion**—Kindness, generosity, and mercy were marks of the samurai. Many insults were forgiven, and in the name of mercy many injuries were not avenged. Much as I tell my students to "consider the source" of the offending remark, samurai also took pity on those they might just as well have killed. Those of a lower station, the poor, and the downtrodden were frequently forgiven for their bitter tongues because of their plight, while a person of equal stature and rank making the same insult would invariably end up testing the metal of the warrior's blade.

The true test of warriors' worth was in their kind and gentle nature. Much as it is today, it was recognized then that the strongest person is the one who can show love, tenderness, and compassion to others. The true signs of weakness and cowardice are the inability to show these virtues, the reliance on displays of physical strength, and the arousing of fear in others.

- **Manners**—Proper manners denote good breeding. To the Japanese, manners are meaningless if they are not displayed for the right reasons. Politeness is more than show today and was for the samurai as well. It was centered in a deep caring and respect for the feelings of the other person. The samurai cultivated such manners as a way to self-improvement and to ease the hardships of daily life.

- **Honesty**—The word of a samurai was incontrovertible. Verbal contracts were the norm because reducing dealings to writing was considered beneath a samurai's dignity. To insist on the swearing of an oath was a paramount insult to the warrior's honor. Honesty and truth were so highly cherished among the samurai that when the feudal system was abolished and many had to resort to lower forms of trade, many were wiped out entirely. They simply were not prepared to enter into commerce where the same codes of ethics and honesty did not apply.

• **Honor**—Honor is defined in the dictionary as "good name or public esteem, merited respect or recognition." Throughout history, countless thousands of soldiers have died over affronts to honor, many times so trivial that those laying down their lives did not understand why they were doing so.

Dishonor, more often than not, took the shape of failure to perform the duties or orders of the feudal lord or superior. The samurai felt a very deep shame in failing at any ordered task. To save a family's name, the warrior often committed ritual seppuku—suicide by disembowelment—either out of shame or at the command of a superior to atone for one's sins. The other more common type of dishonor was the physical attack on female samurai. So strong was their sense of shame in being violated that they would take their own lives rather than permit it, and in their last moments of life, they would tie their feet together as a testimony of their saved chastity.

• **Loyalty**—This was a given among these people. Loyalty to a master was complete until death. Dying in service to one's lord was the highest display of allegiance. The emperor as the embodiment of God on earth came first, the feudal lord second, family third, and vassals last, but not least. Loyalty worked both ways. There was a very strong fatherly role that samurai had for those beneath them as well.

The Aikijujutsu, fencing, and other Jujitsu systems that formed Uyeshiba's roots were derived directly from the ancient samurai arts of hand-to-hand combat. As such, they were much more aggressive in nature, frequently ending in the death of the opponent. They consisted of combinations of strikes, throws, joint locks, kicking, kneeing, choking, and weapons. Little thought was given to the welfare of the attacker when faced in real battle. Even the Aikijujutsu of today is much more brutal than Aikido and routinely teaches "finishing" moves similar to those of the harder martial systems.

From all he had learned, Uyeshiba gleaned what he felt was the best of each to form a new system called Aikibujutsu. It was this unarmed combat system that Uyeshiba, or "O'Sensei" as he was affectionately called, began teaching originally in 1918. This is the system that all his senior disciples originally were taught; a combat/self-defense system derived from various Jujitsu and fencing arts.

According to Yamada and Macintosh (1966), about 1923 O'Sensei had his now famous "spiritual awakening" following a confrontation with a naval cadet who was one of his students. After a one-sided sword battle in which O'Sensei easily dodged the student's blade until the latter became exhausted, O'Sensei is said to have stumbled outside, leaned against a tree, and had a spiritual revelation. He understood the birds as they sang and the intentions of God. The universe is said to have been opened up to him. As a result, he began to change his approach to the martial arts to a more spiritual "Do," or way of life. At the post–World War II conference of the All Japan Budo Federation in 1947, the official announcement was made that Uyeshiba had changed the name of his system to Aikido.

The resulting art form (Aikido, meaning "way of spiritual harmony") is characterized by a profound compassion for the attacker and a desire above all to end the conflict and restore

THE SWORD

No discussion on Aikido would be complete without mention of the importance of the sword. Aikido is based a great deal on principles of sword techniques derived from the Yagi-ryu system of Kenjutsu.

The sword represents the embodiment of the samurai soul and spirit. It represents a symbol of status and rank. The samurai would never be seen outdoors without these weapons at their sides. Even the female samurai would conceal a dirk (dagger) within the bosom for self-defense. When indoors, the swords were displayed in the most prominent spot in the house and were placed at the bedside within easy reach during sleep. The sword was quite often given a proper name and was very nearly worshipped. Even the simplest dirk was afforded great respect. It was a serious insult to the owner to insult the weapon, no matter its condition. If a sword or dagger was found on the floor, the visitor was obliged to walk around it rather than pick it up or offend the owner by stepping over it.

harmony. As a "Do," this art became centered on the philosophical aspects of martial-arts training and its impact on the mental and spiritual development of the individual student. Most of the underlying philosophy came from the Shinto and Shingon Buddhist religions. Aikido is now studied by many as a means of attaining spiritual enlightenment and attaining oneness with the forces of the universe.

The techniques themselves did not change as much as did the intention of performing them. With such a compassionate approach to combat, execution of the techniques became softer, focusing on harmonizing with and controlling the opponent rather than injuring or defeating him. Much more emphasis was placed on the spiritual development of the practitioner than on combat principles.

O'Sensei is said to have had a peculiar habit of stressing different aspects of his art to different students. It is not known whether this was because of a specific interest or pronounced aptitude on the part of the student. His teaching philosophy reflected his attitude toward his senior students. After O'Sensei had taught his senior students all he had to offer, he commanded that they go "find their own Aikido."

So it was that some of his senior students sought their own way. Out of respect for Uyeshiba and the art that gave them their roots, they all kept the name of Aikido and introduced new style names. Among these students were Gozo Shioda (Yoshinkan Aikido), Kenji Tomiki (Tomiki-ryu Aikido), Minoru Hirai (Korindo Aikido), and Minoru Mochizuki, who founded the Yoseikan system of Aikido.

Many branch systems of Aikido exist today, and most were founded by the original senior disciples themselves, like Morihiro Saito and Koichi Tohei. There are also different emphases within systems. Saito emphasizes sword and weapons training, while Tohei, who was the first to bring Aikido to the United States, almost exclusively teaches ki (inner spirit) development. Almost all these branch systems deal with self-defense and the desire to return to the combat roots of Aikibujutsu.

Most Aikido students believe they are studying traditional Aikido and are not aware that there are different systems. The following description of Aikido systems comes from material in *Martial Arts Traditions, History, People* by Corcoran and Farkas.

Other forms of Aikido are taught as well, and I hope that the students of those systems that were not mentioned will pardon my oversight. Whether Hombu Aikido or one of these subsystems, Aikido is a deeply personal study that has a different meaning to each of its students.

MAJOR AIKIDO SYSTEMS

As mentioned previously, Aikido takes many forms and is something different to each person. However, the Aikido systems discussed in the following paragraphs are more prominent and have a larger following than others.

Hombu Aikido. Also known as Uyeshiba Aikido, this is the root system headed by O'Sensei's son Kishomaru, who also heads the International Aikido Federation (IAF). Both the system and the IAF have their headquarters at the Aikikai, or central dojo (school), in the Shinjuku district of Tokyo. This is Aikido as it was practiced after Uyeshiba's spiritual awakening about 1923, as it was when it was officially changed from Aikibujutsu to a "Do" in 1947, and as it was at the time of his death in 1969. It is the main system of Aikido in the world, with a strong following not only in Japan, but in the United States and Europe as well.

Yoshinkan Aikido. Founded by Gozo Shioda, this system seeks to portray the "true" nature of Aikido or, more accurately, the original Aikibujutsu. Shioda was not comfortable with Uyeshiba's religious approach to the martial arts and held to the art's original combat principles. This is considered a "hard" style, putting less emphasis on ki development than other Aikido styles. His purpose is to instill correct technique so the student may find the underlying harmony within the movements. It is represented in the United States by the Aikido Yoshinkai Association and has a strong following both in the United States and in Japan.

Tomiki-ryu Aikido. Kenji Tomiki, a student of both Uyeshiba and Dr. Jigoro Kano's Judo, was also the physical education director of Waseda University in Tokyo. He felt that although Aikido technical variations can easily run into the thousands, they are based on relatively few basic body motions. He undertook development of a simplified version of Aikido that could be easily taught and absorbed by students in colleges and universities. Its primary distinction is that it incorporates elements of competition, or randori, into its practice.

Yoseikan Aikido. Founded by Minoru Mochizuki, Yoseikan Aikido was an attempt by Mochizuki to return to the Aikibujutsu philosophy of combat, while still embracing much of the pacifistic philosophy of O'Sensei. Many who follow this system think that it more closely resembles Jujitsu than it does Aikido. Yoseikan stresses technique over spiritual development. It has been renamed in recent years to Yoseikan Budo.

Nihon Goshin Aikido. Founded by Shodo Morita, this is a six-dan system based upon principles from all the Japanese martial arts. Morita believed that no one art teaches principles that are applicable to each and every situation. This system has been headed by Morita's disciple, Master Richard A. Bowe of New Jersey, since Morita's death in 1962.

OTHER AIKIDO SYSTEMS

The following are some of the lesser-known Aikido systems about which there is not a great deal of information published. These systems, while having their own loyal followings, are small in comparison with the ones listed previously.

- **Shinwa Taido Aikido**—Yoichiro Inoue, another of Uyeshiba's senior disciples, founded this system, which is a blend of sport and self-defense.

- **Otsuki Ryu Aikido**—Founded by Yutaka Otsuki, this system focuses on the self-defense aspects of Aikido. Otsuki was a direct student of O'Sensei.

- **Kobu-jutsu Aikido**—Created by Tetsumis Hoshi, this self-defense system's founder was also a direct student of Uyeshiba.

- **Shin Riaku Heiho Aikido**—Setaro Tanaka, another direct student of the founder, created this self-defense style of Aikido. Some of his students are said to be designing other combat systems that are Aikido based.

- **Yae-ryu Aikido**—A combat style developed by Tanaka student Harunosuke Fukui.

- **Shindo Rokugo Aikido**—Uyeshiba's last direct pupil, Senryuken Noguchi, is the founder of this self-defensive Aikido style.
- **Keijutsukai Aikido**—This system, founded by Thomas Makiyama of Hawaii, stresses practical self-defense applications for people of limited physical capacity.
- **Korindo Aikido**—Founded by Minoru Hirai, another direct disciple of Uyeshiba, this system, like so many others, tries to embrace the original principles and techniques.
- **Tejitsu Aikido**—Based on the techniques of Yoseikan Aikido and the principles of Tomiki-ryu Aikido and founded by Gary Bennett, Tejitsu Aikido is designed for close-quarter combat using minimal footwork.

While many students of the mainstream systems argue that "Aikido is Aikido" and that the systems are not really separate, this is obviously not the case. By teaching different things to different students, O'Sensei saw to it that the skills he brought to the public would continue to grow and mature, making a place for all who wished to participate. In doing so, he showed the true nature of the Grandmaster, not just to perpetuate what currently exists, but to ensure growth and vitality for years to come.

CHAPTER

3

LANGUAGE AND PRINCIPLES OF AIKIDO

ikido is a Japanese martial art, which means that students are obliged to learn and use the terminology of the system, as well as learn the disciplines of the society from which it came. This obligation is partly to respect the art and partly to give students the opportunity to broaden their horizons and learn from another culture. Depending upon the Aikido school you choose, your classes may be conducted in English or in Japanese. This chapter provides the Japanese terms for common words you will encounter and describes the typical Aikido class. This is followed by a list of single terms that appear throughout the book, including those referring to areas of the body and basic techniques. Another list of compound terms gets into a little more detail by providing the technique names found in this book and giving a brief explanation of the execution of the technique. Learning these customs and terms will help you become familiar with the Japanese culture that inspired Aikido and become more proficient when entering the dojo.

The last half of this chapter is devoted to describing the seven basic Aikido principles that will be used throughout the techniques in this book. These principles help to define Aikido and describe how to achieve harmonious self-defense. It is important to understand these principles in order to overcome the human tendency to try to meet force with superior force.

JAPANESE CULTURE

Japanese culture is steeped in tradition going back to the feudal era and beyond. The martial arts themselves derive from the order and traditions of the samurai, which were presented in chapter 2. The traditional honor and respect for one's superior is of utmost importance in everyday Japanese life, as well as in the dojo or training hall.

One never uses someone's first name unless very well acquainted, just as Westerners address each other by surnames such as Mr. Jones or Ms. Jones. When greeting one another, people use a traditional bow from the waist, much like the Western tradition of shaking hands. The same traditions are followed in the dojo. Relations between the instructor and the student are very formal and respectful. Teachers are always addressed as "sensei," or teacher, and students, depending upon the school, are usually addressed as Mr. Smith or Miss Smith, and so on.

GENERAL TERMS

During your time in Aikido training, you will be exposed to, and expected to understand, certain terminology and commands. If you do not make an effort to learn these terms, you will be out of place and out of sync with the rest of the class.

Aikidoist or *Aikidoka* means someone who practices or studies the art of Aikido. The training hall is known as the *dojo*. The main school of any system is known as the *Hombu dojo*. All Aikido instructors are addressed as *sensei* or teacher. Master-

PRONUNCIATION GUIDELINES

SHORT VOWELS

- "a" as in father
- "e" as in pen
- "i" as in seen
- "o" as in old
- "u" as in true, unless following an *s*, then it is silent (an example would be "suteki," pronounced "steki")

Long vowels have the same pronunciation as short vowels, except that they are held double in length.

VOWEL COMBINATIONS

- "ai" as an "i" like alive
- "ae" as a short "o" and long "a" as "ah-ay"
- "ao" as a short "a" and long "o" as "ah-oh"
- "ei" as an "a" like day
- "ou" as an "o" like boat
- "au" as an "ou" like out

CONSONANTS

Most consonants are pronounced the same as in English, except the *r*, which is pronounced more like "l," and the *n* followed by *b, m,* or *p,* which is pronounced as "m." Double consonants are pronounced as two distinct letters except for the following blended sounds:

- "ch" as in chime
- "sh" as in ship
- "ts" as in cats

level instructors are titled as ***renshi*** or ***shihan*** but are always addressed directly as sensei. Grandmasters are titled as ***hanshi*** but still addressed as sensei.

In the dojo, a uniform, or ***gi,*** must be worn at all times. This consists of a white jacket and pants tied at the waist with an ***obi,*** or belt. Many Aikido practitioners wear the ***hakama,*** or divided skirt, over the pants. It is floor length and designed to hide the motion of the feet. All persons entering or leaving the dojo are expected to bow *(rei)* in respect for the training hall, the instructor, and the other students. The sidebar below lists other common rules of the training hall.

AIKIDO CLASS

The typical 2-hour Aikido class will follow a similar format to the one described here. At the beginning of class, students line up

COMMON RULES OF THE DOJO

1. Golden Rule of the Dojo: Throw others as you would have others throw you!

2. Always give way to a high belt. This means letting a higher-ranked individual go first, have a seat, lead the conversation, and so on. (Here a "high belt" means anyone outranking you.)

3. Respect the rank of others, and they will in turn respect your rank. Someday you will be the high belt and will expect the respect that comes with it.

4. Respect the property of others. Do not borrow or use another's training equipment without permission.

5. Respect the training hall and always leave it the way you found it. Clean up any mess before leaving.

6. Wear proper, clean uniforms at all times after achieving belt rank.

7. Never wear shoes in the training area. Walking through the training area with shoes on can track foreign objects onto the floor, which could cut the feet.

8. Observe traditional bowing at all times. Bowing is an expression of respect for your instructors, peers, and the training hall.

9. Always remember that your partner's safety is *your* responsibility. Your partner is there not only to train but also to assist you in your training. Treat your partner with courtesy, respect, and appreciation.

10. Never use profanity, sexist remarks, or lewd or suggestive actions.

facing the instructor, with the senior-rank student to the far right and all others in descending order of rank lining up on his or her left. Students who are not properly dressed for class lose the status of their place in line and must fall in at the end of the line. Visitors with rank in other systems are permitted to take a place in line according to their rank, and beginning visitors are the last in line. Two people of the same rank determine their position in line by time in grade or, if that's equal, by age.

To open the class, the senior-rank student in attendance gives the commands *"kiotsuke,"* meaning to come to attention, and **"rei,"** meaning bow with respect. All students then bow to the instructor. Many schools perform the bow from a kneeling or Japanese sitting position called *seiza* instead of standing. In seiza, the knees are slightly apart and the big toes of each foot are overlapped behind you.

Students are then instructed to spread out and begin their warm-up exercises, which are detailed in chapter 5. After the warm-ups, the class is split into pairs, and each student will assume one of two roles, either that of *uke* the attacker or *tori* the defender. The command *"hajime,"* or begin, will be issued. Each student will spend half the class as the attacker and half as the defender, performing the techniques outlined by the instructor. At the end of class or any time a break in the practice is called, the instructor will give the command *"matte,"* or stop and pay attention. Partners will face each other and bow, line up, and close the class the same as it began.

TECHNIQUE TERMS

SINGLE TERMS

Japanese	English
ashi	leg or ankle
ate	attack
atemi	strike
chigai	with distinction
daoshi	take-down
do	body or trunk

dosokyu	single-hand (cross-body)
gaeshi	turn out
gari	reap
gyaku	reverse
hana	nose
hineri	twist
hishigi	straight bar
ippo	cross-body
kaiten	rotary
katate	single hand
kote	wrist
kubi	neck
mauri	circular
mukae	opposing
mune	body
nage	throw
O	major
otoshi	drop
ryote	two-hand
shiho	four-directional
shomen	frontal
soto	outer
tori	hold or capture
tsuki	punch
tsume	claw
uchi	blow or strike
ude	arm
ushiro	rear or from behind
waza	technique
yokomen	roundhouse
yuki	bravery

COMPOUND TERMS

Japanese	English
ashi-waza	Leg technique—Ankle is blocked to prevent the attacker from regaining balance. Throw is executed by pulling arm to the side.
do-gaeshi	Trunk turn—Arm is extended across uke's throat, and take-down is achieved by turning the upper body at the waist and sweeping the arm to the rear.
dosokyu-katate-tori	Single-hand cross-body hold—A grabbing attack in which uke grabs tori's right wrist with his right hand (or grabs tori's left wrist with his left hand) by reaching across the body when standing face-to-face.
gyaku-ate	Reverse attack—Wrist lock is applied with the wrist turned inward with the palm toward the wrist.
gyaku-katate-tori	Reversed single-hand hold—A grabbing attack in which uke grabs the same-side wrist of tori on the palm side of the wrist.
hana-nage	Nose throw—A rear sweeping technique in which balance is broken by sweeping two fingers up under the nose, then sweeping the hand to the rear and down.
ikkyo	First technique—Tori locks uke's arm in a fully extended straight position (called an armbar) and exerts downward pressure on the elbow.
kaiten-nage	Rotary throw—A forward throw or projection in which pressure is applied to the back of the head, forcing it down, while the arm is forced back-

ward and upward, causing uke to be rolled forward head over heels. Also known as "wheel throw." (Also called *ude-hineri*.)

katate-tori   Single-hand hold—Grabbing attack performed by reaching straight out from the body and grabbing the same-side wrist of the defender.

kote-gaeshi   Wrist turnout—Wrist lock achieved by twisting the wrist toward the body, then out at a 45-degree angle. Used to control or throw.

kote-kudaki   Wrist break—Wrist lock achieved by twisting arm, then applying pressure to wrist or elbow.

kubi-waza   Neck technique—Similar to ashi-waza in which arm is pulled to the side, but balance is broken by attacking the pressure point under the jawbone midway between chin and temperomandibular joint.

mae-ryote-tori   Straight two-hand wrist grab.

mukae-daoshi   Opposing arm take-down—Scissors-like motion in which upper arm applies pressure to face and sweeps to the rear, while lower arm presses inward to the small of the back, resulting in a rear throw.

mune-tsuki   Body punch—A hand strike to the body directed generally at the belly or solar plexus, thrown either as a straight punch or similar to an uppercut.

o-soto-gari   Major outer reap—Uke is forced off-balance so that balance is on one foot, then that foot is firmly swept out from underneath the body.

robuse   See *ikkyo*.

ryote-ippo-tori	Two-hand cross-body grab—Cross-body grip in which uke grabs tori's arm with a hold similar to that used for gripping a baseball bat.
sankyo	Third technique—Tori locks uke's arm in a box shape, then throws him.
shiho-nage	Four-corner throw—A wrist throw executed using the arm for leverage, with the attacker landing in a backfall.
shomen-ate	Frontal attack—A rear throw executed by exerting pressure up under the chin and pushing to the rear.
shomen-uchi	Straight-face punch—A lead-hand punch or rear cross that is delivered in a straight line, as opposed to a hook or roundhouse.
tsume-otoshi	Claw drop—Similar to ashi-waza, except that the balance is broken by literally trying to grasp the collarbone with a "claw" closing motion. Arm is then pulled to the side without blocking the ankle.
ude-garami	Entangled arm lock.
ude-hineri	Arm twist—See *kaiten-nage.*
ude-hishigi	Straight armbar—Arm is outstretched to the side of uke's body and held at chest level where pressure is applied to the back of the elbow, forcing the attacker into a painful armbar. Uke can either be controlled here or forced to the floor.
ushiro-katate-tori	Rear two-hand hold—A grabbing attack in which uke is standing directly behind tori and reaches straight forward and grabs both arms at the wrists.

ushiro-tori	Bear hug attack from behind.
yokomen-uchi	Circular or roundhouse strike—Performed with a big hooking motion. Often called a "cowboy punch" because of its use on American TV westerns.
yuki-chigai	See *sankyo*.

BASIC AIKIDO PRINCIPLES

The principles discussed here differentiate Aikido from other martial-art systems, particularly hard styles such as Karate and Taekwondo. In order to practice Aikido, one must learn to flow with and blend with an attack, just as a sapling bends under the weight of snow or with a strong wind. It survives because it is flexible and goes along with the more powerful force rather than trying to resist it. Many a strong oak breaks under the same pressure because it is rigid and unyielding. When meeting force with force, the stronger prevails; when giving way and redirecting force, the weak can overcome the strong.

Many systems other than Aikido, such as Judo, Jujitsu, and Kung-fu, teach some of the same principles presented here. These other systems, however, do not rely totally on the principles as does Aikido. Aikido is designed to be most effective for people of smaller stature and less strength. It is only by using these principles that they can hope to overcome the big and powerful. These principles are found in all Aikido systems.

YIELD (YOTTO)

To properly practice Aikido, you must first learn not to resist an attack but instead to yield to it or "submit" to your attacker's force. Nonresistance is the key to overcoming your opponent's attack. There is no need to meet force with force. It is not necessary to overcome through overpowering the enemy. By simply redirecting your enemy's force, she will, many times, actually throw herself with little help on your part.

Those of you familiar with firearms know what happens when the bullet from a high-powered rifle grazes a small sapling on the way to the target. It is deflected from the intended path and misses the prey. The same thing happens when an Aikidoist submits to an attack. In deflecting or redirecting an opponent's attack, the student will gain complete control of the attacker and the situation. By yielding to and redirecting the opponent's motion, the practitioner draws the attacker off-balance. Once the balance is broken, a controlling technique or throw can be easily executed.

For example, if an attacker pushes you, he expects to be met with resistance or at least the weight of your body. If you move just as he pushes forward toward you, his own force will carry him past where you were standing, taking him off-balance.

No Mind (Mushin)

In each self-defense situation, it is necessary to gain control mentally first. If your mind is properly prepared to deal with a confrontation, then you will have no anger. Anger has no place in a defense situation. Anger will cause a loss of awareness and will cause you to make mistakes.

A mind at peace will not react with aggression but with clarity of thought. Many fights have been avoided and many lives saved by one person's ability to remain calm and not react to the aggressive actions of another.

The state of mushin (literally translated as "no mind") is the highest goal to which an Aikido student, or any martial-art student for that matter, can aspire. Reaching a state of no mind is more than mere perfection of technique. It is more than having memorized the proper sequence or pattern. It is more than instinct.

Mushin is a level that a student must enter normally before attaining master's ranking (fourth dan or higher), in which response to attack or danger seems to be automatic. The mind basically shuts down at a conscious level and lets the subconscious take over to produce a totally *clear mind.* This clear mind processes information very quickly and employs instantaneous *rational thought.* It is not unusual for practitioners at this level to have no recall immediately after a confrontation. It can frequently take hours and the input of witnesses to piece together the details of how the attacker was disabled. It is a commonly known fact that it takes 5,000 repetitions of any variation to make it instinctive. It is only through years of practice and repetitions that such a state can be achieved.

The martial artist who has reached this level will never have to worry about overreacting, hurting someone by accident, or using an inappropriate response if surprised. Mushin is a state of empty-mindedness, free from conscious thought, free from anger, and free from prejudice. It is a form of autopilot that instantly assesses the situation, the dangers involved, and the measures needed to survive, that chooses from the vast array of stored knowledge, and that executes the one perfect response. This response could be as simple as merely ducking an attack or as complex as employing near-deadly force.

If you have been around the martial-arts world for long, you have undoubtedly seen or heard of the following sequence of events. A newcomer or student from a rival school throws a surprise punch at the instructor, whose response is to do nothing . . . not even flinch. The would-be attacker's response is to ridicule the instructor for failing to react to the "deadly" attack.

To the untrained eye, this may seem true. To a person who understands mushin, it is perfectly natural. The instructor's response to a punch that did not land was to do nothing. In the wink of an eye, the instructor assessed the situation and reasoned that this person would not dare attack in someone else's school in front of all the students. The instructor also determined that the punch would probably be pulled short of contact, and he formulated a "plan B" reaction in case this judgment was in error. It was not. This well-trained instructor could easily have killed the student, but there was no real attack, no real danger, and therefore no need to respond—mushin.

WEAKNESS (YOWASA)

Weakness, gentleness, and passiveness are not terms usually associated with martial-arts training. Indeed, most people associate training in the arts with developing awesome power, building muscle mass, getting into top physical condition, improving endurance, and toughening their bodies. These are all admirable goals and are very valuable for the students of most martial arts.

Aikido, however, is very different in this respect. Aikido is much more scientific in its approach. It uses the weakness of the human body against itself by attacking those points with only a slight amount of pressure. Students are constantly amazed that they can learn to cause much more pain with just the touch of a finger than they can using all their might. This technique is something any student can learn, but it takes time and practice. For example, later in the text the technique called kote-gaeshi is illustrated using a two-handed grip. By knowing the exact weak point on the back of the hand, the same technique can actually be applied more effectively using the pressure of one finger.

By design, Aikido is well suited to men and women with less strength because it requires no muscle power to execute. Power actually works against the practitioner and makes the techniques ineffective. The hardest lesson many students have to learn is to turn off their strength and be gentle. It is totally inconceivable to most students that all the muscles they have spent a lifetime building are of absolutely no use in this type of self-defense. This is not to say that physically strong men and women cannot properly learn Aikido. It is just a matter of unlearning the "power response" or the tendency to use brute strength. Although this principle may take some effort, anyone can master it.

That the largest opponent can be thrown by applying pressure with just one finger is not a feat of magic or spiritual force. We simply have had many years of practice in how to apply pressure to the body in its weakest spots. The result can be immobilizing and extremely painful to your attacker with almost no effort at all!

KI (POWER)

The term *ki* is one that many Aikido students do not find easy to understand. According to Eastern philosophy, ki is the human spirit inhabiting a flesh body. It is part of a higher spiritual force of which the entire universe is made up. Ki, or as the Chinese say, chi, is a flow of energy that comes from the universe and returns to the universe. It is the life force that inhabits our bodies at birth and returns to the cosmos when our physical bodies die. Humans have a trinity of existence: a mind, a soul, and a spirit. The spirit is ki or chi.

Some schools are more involved with ki development than others. To many students, ki seems to be mystical and even contrary to Biblical principles. To appreciate ki, one must have an understanding of the principles of Eastern religion, the concept of reincarnation, and the existence of each of us as an immortal spiritual being capable of many physical lives.

Many people do not practice ki power. They believe their power does not lie in a mystical universal force that can be channeled through their bodies. Instead, they believe it is simple human physiology and leverage. Therefore, their studies revolve around kinesiology and not around the spiritual powers. A more scientifically based explanation centers on the idea that all functions of the body are a result of electrical stimulation of nerves. The human body simply operates on electrical power. No muscle can move, no sight can be seen, no sound heard, no touch felt, and no thought processed without it.

As we all know, electricity flows between contact points by way of some sort of conductor. When the circuit is complete, the device at the end of the circuit, whether a light, a motor, or a finger, will react to the stimulation. In the body, this electrical force can be controlled or focused by the brain at any given second. Through training, this energy can be focused into specific parts of the body and can generate what seems to be mysterious and miraculous feats of strength. These amazing demonstrations of ki are merely selective uses of internal muscle control generated from within. The superhuman feats that are seen are merely an outward manifestation of this internal force.

Take, for example, the well-known demonstration by the Aikido instructor who seems to be rooted to the ground. Even though a much larger, stronger, and more powerful man attempts to lift the teacher, he cannot. This is commonly taught to be a display of extending one's ki toward the ground.

Here's the real secret. It is all done with muscle control, by affecting the flow of the body's electricity. While standing relaxed with your feet about shoulder-width apart, take a breath and push down internally as if you were trying to move your bowels. By pushing downward with your diaphragm, you are directing your internal energy toward the floor, effectively becoming dead weight.

A favorite exercise that my instructors and I perform is something I call "soft palm breaking." I place my hand, palm upward, on a stack of boards. With no windup or external display of power, I am able to break the boards by merely flipping the hand over and driving through. The power is generated internally rather than externally. The power of the entire body is directed downward to a point below that of the boards and is committed toward that point by one focused motion. Those who are used to breaking by brute force are amazed at this exercise because there is never even a one-inch windup. Similar in execution to Bruce Lee's famous one-inch punch, all the power is internally (electrically) generated.

No matter how you choose to believe that it works, there is an energy within the human body that can be manipulated. To succeed in Aikido training, you must learn to control that energy. It does not mean you must become a Buddhist and believe in something that is contrary to your religion or beliefs. The energy is simply there, no matter what you want to call it, and the energy may be used to help you master your Aikido skills.

CIRCLE (EN)

The circle is an all-important part of Aikido. The concept of circular (mauri) motion is the very basis of Aikido techniques. Although it is necessary in combat to use much smaller motions than in the dojo, the circle is still of the utmost importance.

To fully understand the importance of the circle to martial-arts training, think about the operation of the wheel. As the wheel turns, notice the way the axle or center of the circle actually seems to rotate fairly slowly compared with the outer edge of the circle.

Just as the wheel has a center, the Aikido practitioner becomes the center of the circle. As the practitioner controls the opponent and begins to move in a circular pattern, the attacker is forced to move at a much greater speed to keep up with the center of the circle. This, of course, is impossible, resulting in the attacker's balance being broken and allowing the defender to easily throw the attacker to the ground or otherwise render her harmless with a lock of some kind. The use of circular motion requires no strength. Its use must rely on the lack of strength because circular motion cannot be accomplished by brute force.

LINE (SEN)

Linear motion also has its place in Aikido training. Unlike harder systems that use linear motion to stop an opponent's motion or force, in Aikido linear motion is used as more of a push or pull to break an attacker's balance and help facilitate a throw or help maneuver him into a joint lock or break. For example, suppose a person lunges at you in a straight line. If you move out of the way and give him a slight push or pull in the same direction he is

already going, he will lose his balance and fall or provide you with
an opening to execute a counterlock or throw.

BREAKING THE BALANCE (KUZUSHI)

Balance is the ability to keep your body in an upright and stable
position against the forces of gravity, motion, and kinetic energy.
Two ways of breaking the balance in Aikido are happo-no-kuzushi
and hando-no-kuzushi.

Happo-no-kuzushi is performed by breaking the balance in one
direction. Many of the techniques that I teach seem to naturally
fit this method, and, indeed, many of the upper-level techniques
that rely on nothing more than attacking a pressure point to
achieve kuzushi actually do move the attacker in one direction
only. For instance, if I apply pressure to the tip of your nose, your
natural reaction would be to lean backward to try to get away from
the pressure. Once you have broken your own balance to the rear,
I would simply help you along in the direction you have already
chosen, and throw you to the rear.

In hando-no-kuzushi, my approach differs considerably from
many other Aikido systems. The original intent of this type of
balance breaking is to lead your opponent and have her balance
broken in one direction, then to reverse your motion as she is
trying to recover her balance to take her farther in another
direction. The theory is that when your opponent is trying to
regain balance, it is very easy to make her overcompensate. You
should try to take advantage of this overcompensation.

The method portrayed in this book is different in that the initial
balance-breaking motion is a good atemi, or strike, that dazes the
opponent. The throw relies on the fact that the assailant's balance
is now upset and unstable no matter what direction I should
choose. There is no need to lead first in one direction and then
reverse it. Any motion that is applied to the assailant's balance
will result in a throw because the equilibrium is now gone. This
approach may seem to some not to fit in this classification of
kuzushi, but, even though extremely subtle, it is actually breaking the balance twice.

Balance can be broken in eight directions that are similar to the
major directional points on a compass. These are front, rear, left,
right, left rear, right rear, left front, and right front. If north is

considered rear, the directions would correspond with the compass points as south, north, west, east, northeast, northwest, southeast, and southwest. These are only the major directions; there are as many possible directions as there are points on a compass. A throw can be initiated anywhere within the 360-degree area of the circle.

Different schools and systems have different methods of breaking the balance. Some Aikido schools and instructors teach striking as a primary method of breaking the balance while others do not. Some systems have few strikes, and those strikes they do teach are more to distract the attacker's attention than to break the balance or serve as a knockout blow. The primary method of breaking the balance is to draw the attacker off balance, then make a quick directional change and reverse the motion so that the attacker actually has a tendency to walk out from under his own body. Some systems do not employ pressure-point attacks while some others do. Poking a finger into a sensitive part of someone's body, for example just under the jawbone along the neck, is a very effective way to break the balance because the attacker rocks backward to avoid the pain.

What is important is to evaluate this and all material on their own merits and accept the methods presented both here and elsewhere as points of view worth considering. There are many different styles of Aikido, just as there are many different styles of Karate or Jujitsu. Each has its own area of specialization and emphasis. What is important to one style is not so important to another.

Aikido has no aggressive techniques. Instead, it employs strategic and intelligent use of defensive skills to overcome an attack. While the dojo dictates that you should never cause injury to an opponent, sometimes this is unavoidable. The next chapter will familiarize you with the adaptations necessary for a street confrontation and the legal parameters of self-defense.

CHAPTER

4

USING AIKIDO
IN SELF-
DEFENSE

The use of Aikido, as of any other martial art, must be tempered by common sense and a thorough understanding of the legal ramifications involved. Just as police officers have a duty *not* to use a gun unless their life or that of an innocent person is threatened, so the trained martial artist has a responsibility not to use deadly force without just cause. In addition to describing the legal limits of self-defense, this chapter introduces the combat adaptations of traditional Aikido moves that will be highlighted throughout the rest of the book. You'll learn that the techniques detailed later have been adapted from the original form to portray how best to apply them in a street combat situation with limited space to maneuver. It is my hope that the beginner and experienced Aikidoka as well will find these adaptations both interesting and useful.

JUSTIFIABLE FORCE

Many martial artists believe that they understand the concept of self-defense and are shocked to realize that what they have been taught about the legalities in a self-defense situation has been in error. The concept of self-defense passed on to many martial artists by their instructors has been out of line with what their actual rights are when defending themselves or their loved ones. This is partially the fault of the instructors and, in a very large way, the fault of the media in the United States.

Most people get a great deal of their self-defense philosophy from what they see on television, in the movies, in video games, and in print. All too often in these media, the treatment of a person's right to self-defense is based on beating the attacker into an unconscious state. Worse yet, the idea that we have the inalienable right to punish the assailant has been drilled into our heads by countless acts of violence on television and on the big screen.

What people do not realize while watching martial-arts movies is that violence sells. Those movies are not an accurate portrayal of what the star would actually do in a real conflict. The truth of the matter is that these superstars, even though they would never act this way in real life, defend, rationalize, and even promote extra violence in their films to please the viewing public's media-fed addiction to violence and keep their ratings up.

Martial-arts training is not about beating up the bad guy or punishing the criminal. The very worst depiction of the misuse of martial-arts skills is the "coup de grace," or finishing blow. Originally meant to be a death blow to stop the suffering of a mortally wounded opponent, this has been shown time after time as the preferred end to all physical confrontations. How many times have you seen, in the movies or on prime-time television, the "good guy" beat the "bad guy" to the point where he can no longer fight, stand, or put up any type of resistance? What is *always* the next thing that happens? The so-called good guy will give the attacker anything from a look of disgust to a derogatory remark, then calmly proceed to punch or kick him in the head to knock him out cold. Some video games even encourage killing the helpless victim after the fight has ended.

If the martial artist is guided by what has been learned from the media, that person will probably wind up in jail after a physical encounter. The only right you have to defend yourself is to *neutralize the attack,* nothing more. You may protect yourself, but not at the expense of another life. If you are not properly trained, there may indeed come a day when you have to kill in order to not be killed, but on that day, you had better be able to prove that you had no other choice.

If properly trained, the martial artist will never have to kill to survive, unless in a war. An untrained person usually uses deadly force because he lacks knowledge about other ways to survive. Martial-arts training, on the other hand, should focus first and foremost on conflict avoidance through a heightened sense of awareness, then on defending oneself. Remember, your first obligation is to run if you can!

I have seen so many youngsters at tournaments who have been taught to apply a killing blow as a matter of course at the end of any fight. This is not the fault of the child. Likewise, it is not the fault of the instructor, but the fault of a basic weakness in the system itself. Sadly, the case may be that the instructor knows no other options to guarantee the end of a fight or, because of an erroneous sense of personal honor, will not teach a student to run. Students do not come up with these concepts on their own; they must be taught. In the same way, teachers teach what they have been taught.

The legalities of self-defense are rather simple. First, you may use equal force to repel an attack. If a person punches you, you may not stab that person. Second, if your attacker breaks off the attack or can no longer continue, you must cease also. This means that if a person punches you, turns, and walks away, you have no legal right to go after that person and continue the fight. Finally, you may not kill your opponent unless you are convinced that you or your loved one will surely die if you do not and unless you know of no other way out. What this means to the trained martial artist is this: If you know of another technique you could have used to end the confrontation without killing your opponent, you had better have used it, or you may have to face going to prison.

COMBAT ADAPTATIONS

The dojo all too seldom addresses the need for adaptation of the prescribed execution of each technique. Indeed, instructors often censure a student who asks questions about how a certain technique would be done in a situation that is different from those trained for. The student who has the courage to ask a valid question of this sort should be praised and recognized for her foresight. These are exactly the type of concerns that must be addressed in order to succeed in actual combat.

In actual combat, as opposed to training, there is almost never enough room to maneuver or drastically redirect your opponent's attack. Techniques requiring footwork may have to be shortened, perhaps by getting rid of the footwork entirely. Hard stylists would not be able to use their big, flashy high kicks because there is just not enough room.

The other important issue that must be addressed is that most schools have a tendency to train for show or competition. For example, most schools teach their students to pull their punches short of contact. Even when sparring, the rules mandate such light contact that the person receiving the punch never has to deal with a full-out attack that is meant to do *maximum* damage. Although pulling the punch on the surface seems to be a logical safety precaution, it causes two problems. The student never learns the proper distance for the punch, which means that it falls short in actual combat, and the student learns to block punches that are never intended to make contact. I have personally known high-belt hard stylists who, being used to pulling their punches and kicks a little bit short in training, have been beaten by street brawlers before they made the adjustment and got their distance down.

To properly prepare for real combat, training methods should be adapted to simulate real combat *all the time!* It is not enough to devote a few minutes of each class to self-defense practice. Worse yet, some instructors never touch on it at all. It is for this reason that all my Tejitsu Aikido students, from white belt upward, learn how to deal with strikes intended for contact and penetration. The strikes begin slowly and progress in speed and power as the student's ability to handle them increases. This concept is rarely seen in *any* martial art.

The following photo sequences illustrate the differences between dojo form and combat-adapted form when facing the same attack.

KOTE-GAESHI FACE-PUNCH DEFENSE—TRAINING

Against a face punch, tori uses a cross step to get to the outside of the strike and parries the strike, making contact at the wrist (a). Turning the hand over quickly (b), tori grabs the attacking wrist and begins a 360-degree pivot (c-e), sweeping uke along with him and breaking the balance as he redirects the attack. With uke now off-balance, tori begins another 180-degree pivot back the other way, flipping uke into the air, completely off his feet, and landing him in a sidefall position (f). Note that a full 180-degree pivot is not always necessary, depending on how off-balance uke is.

KOTE-GAESHI FACE-PUNCH DEFENSE—TRAINING
(CONTINUED)

KOTE-GAESHI FACE-PUNCH DEFENSE—COMBAT

Against a face punch, tori parries the punch with a rear-hand parry while simultaneously executing a vertical punch to uke's ribs (a). He then grabs the attacker's wrist with his left hand and turns it over so the back of the hand is toward his own chest (b). Tori caps the hand with his right hand (c) and, while holding it close to his chest, steps through with his right foot, taking the fist out at a 45-degree angle (d), resulting in a controlled throw (e).

KOTE-GAESHI FACE-PUNCH DEFENSE—COMBAT
(CONTINUED)

STANDING YOUR GROUND

The first variation that must be made is to stand your ground, which does not mean to stand your ground on the street and not retreat but rather to stand your ground in training. This is not a matter of personal preference but is a fact of life on the street. Most attacks won't come when you have half an acre of room to move. An attacker will invariably try to trap you in an area where you can neither move nor escape. You *must* therefore learn to perform your techniques as though your back were to the wall *all* the time. Whether you are caught between parked cars, in a public rest room, in an elevator, or in a phone booth, you have to be able to adapt your techniques to work anywhere.

As you can see from the illustrations, the dojo version requires a big step to the outside to avoid the oncoming strike. If you have no room on that side because of your surroundings, you will have no choice but to stand your ground and use the combat version that prepares you for just that situation.

BREAKING THE BALANCE

Along with standing your ground, you must also learn to break your opponent's balance without the use of large pivots, which requires a total rethinking of the principles assumed to make Aikido moves work. It is not the huge pivots and directional changes that make the techniques work but rather the simple fact that the techniques themselves can work from a totally static position as long as the balance is broken. This can be done by redirecting your opponent, counterstrikes, or pressure-point manipulation. In the combat version, you will see how the balance is broken by the use of a well-placed vertical punch to the floating ribs, which dazes the attacker and facilitates your throw.

Redirecting Your Opponent. To redirect your opponent, you must first deflect his attack. If you have no room to move, you can't redirect his attack by directional changes and pivots. Instead, you must learn to parry his attack with a gentle deflecting blow. This is not to say that we are going to revert to the hard blocking of other systems, but much as a sapling can deflect the path of a bullet from its intended target, a soft parry can deflect a blow away from your face or body. How can an aggressor be moved without using his force or weight against him? The answer is to make him cooperative with a strike or kick to a sensitive area of the body, which causes enough pain not only to daze the attacker but also to break the balance as well.

The parry used in the combat method is nearly the same as that used in the training version. The difference is that in the combat method, the student is accustomed to not being able to get out of the way and knows that the parry does not need the outside step to be effective. Basically, you redirect your opponent's attack rather than evade it as shown in the training method.

Counterstrikes and "Softening Blows." Many systems use blows that are primarily distracting in nature, but real combat calls for real blows. The strikes illustrated in this book are defensive in nature and are never intended to cause serious harm of any kind, but they are much more than a distraction. They are softening blows that daze the attacker, break his balance, and give you time to set up and execute your technique rather than feints that distract the attacker to give you time to maneuver to the outside.

Softening blows, while not used in response to an aggressive strike, are nonetheless responsive to an attack. Any type of grab is just as much of an attack as a punch or kick. All these concepts will be addressed in detail in the following chapter. A counterstrike is a strike in response to a strike—any punch, palmstrike, or kick thrown while an opponent is throwing a strike. Its purpose is to cut off the attack by "beating your attacker to the punch."

Pressure-Point Manipulation. This involves applying pressure to any vulnerable part of the body such as under the chin, along the jawbone, against the tip of the nose, or on the back of the elbow. Pressure-point manipulation is especially effective when you are being attacked in a small space and don't have room to land a good strike. This technique requires virtually no strength.

PICKING THE LANDING SITE

A generally accepted Aikido axiom states that once you have your opponent off-balance and have maneuvered her for the throw, let her fall where she wants and merely control her into the fall. Such a practice must be thrown out in a real combat situation. *Never* let an assailant pick the spot on which to fall.

Survival in a street situation will quite often hinge on how hard a fall your opponent takes. If you have the choice of dropping the attacker on a grassy area he is reaching for or dropping him on the concrete or worse, *do not be nice!* When working in such a small area, control must be complete from beginning to end. Remember, the harder they fall, the less the chance that they will get back up, which means that you will have to do it all over again. The purpose in a self-defense situation is to end the confrontation within a few seconds and escape without injury to yourself and with *minimum* injury to the attacker.

Using the controlled throw shown in the combat method, you can assure that your assailant has a hard landing coming, which should put a stop to the attack.

POSTURE

The other key issue that must be addressed is that of posture, or body position, during a throw. This is closely related to the previous section in that by letting the attacker decide where to fall, he will almost inevitably pull you off-balance with his body weight.

Being off-balance puts you in the *most* dangerous situation in Aikido. We have all seen it, even among the highest ranks. The throw is executed, and your attacker tries to direct his landing; you try to maintain a grip and end up bent over at the waist, as shown in the training method. Stop and think about this for a moment. Trying to be gentle with the attacker and letting him fall where he wants results in an opponent who is not stunned. Also, you are bent over at the waist trying to hold on, and you are in serious danger of getting kicked in the face.

An upright body position, as in the combat method, *must* be maintained at all times in order to stay out of range of the attacker's feet. If your attacker knows how to fall, you run the risk of being injured. It is much better to simply bend at the knees and lower your body position while maintaining a straight back than to bend over and put your face in range of the attacker's feet. If you are performing kote-gaeshi, for example, you have both hands committed to your grip and, subsequently, nothing available with which to block.

With the recent rise in popularity of heavy grappling systems such as Gracie Jujitsu, there is even more danger. People who study these systems not only are proficient at taking a fall but also are quite skilled at taking you with them if you lose control of their body for even a split second. These skilled fighters will sense that you do not have controlling power in your throw, and they will be able to reverse the situation by pulling you to the ground. Once there, you will be choked unconscious in a matter of seconds.

As you can see, practicing Aikido on the street can be quite different from what you learned in the dojo. For that matter, the same is true with all martial arts. With any martial art, room to maneuver is one of the biggest concerns when adapting your techniques to self-defense. If a student has not been taught how to maneuver in small spaces, he could be in big trouble. Street fighters are smart and will always try to back you into a corner.

The next chapter will show you how to effectively get ready to practice your art and protect yourself from injury. You will also learn the most important lesson of all—how to fall!

CHAPTER
5

WORKOUT
PREPARATION

The warm-up exercises and breakfall practice in this chapter are essential parts of Aikido practice and are usually peformed at the beginning of every class. On the surface, breakfall practice may not seem to be a logical part of the warm-ups, but practicing these falls is an important part of workout preparation. How better to get loosened up for your partner who will immediately begin throwing you on the ground?

WARM-UPS

As with any form of physical exercise, it is necessary to first warm up your muscles to avoid the possibility of injury. Most of the work done in this form of Aikido training is upper-body related, so this is where the primary focus is directed.

WRISTS

Two basic warm-up exercises are designed for the wrist area. These are very important because the wrists absorb most of the force of these techniques.

In the first photo, you will see how the kote-gaeshi grip is used to loosen up the wrist area for your workout. Place your right hand at chest level with the palm turned toward you and the fingers pointed straight up. Grip your right hand with your left hand, placing the left-hand thumb between the right-hand little finger and ring finger, and wrapping the left-hand fingers around the base of the right hand. Apply pressure to the wrist, turning it in toward the shoulder at a 45-degree angle until you feel discomfort, then release. Repeat this movement 10 times for each wrist.

The stretch shown in the second photo begins with the hands held at chest level with the forearms parallel to the floor. Grab the right hand with the left hand around the base of the thumb, and bring both elbows toward each other as you raise the hands to chin level, stretching the muscles of the wrist and forearm, then release. Repeat 10 times for each wrist.

SHOULDERS AND UPPER BACK

A simple yet effective exercise to loosen up the deltoids (shoulder girdle) and trapezius muscles (triangle-shaped muscles stretching from the neck down across the shoulder blades) is to make big, full arm circles with both arms extended, getting the largest range of motion possible. First make circles forward and then backward 20 times each.

HEAD AND NECK

With your arms at your sides, drop your chin to touch your chest and hold for 20 seconds. Then drop the head back (but do not hyperextend the neck) and hold for 20 seconds. Finally, tilt your head to each side toward your shoulders, holding for 20 seconds on each side. Repeat each stretch 5 times.

LEGS, HIPS, AND GROIN

Starting with the legs spread more than shoulder-width apart, point one toe out to the side, lower the weight out over that knee, and stretch, trying to bring the other knee as close to the floor as possible. Do not bounce with this motion; it is to be a slow, gradual stretch. Repeat on the other side, holding the stretches for a count of 20.

BREAKFALLS

Learning to fall is the most important concept and the first thing taught in Aikido training. If you are knocked to the ground and injured, the confrontation is over. You must learn to protect yourself in a fall so as to be able to return to the fight.

Aikido practice consists of many throws, so the only way to safely practice the techniques is to actually practice throwing your opponent. You and your training partner must be comfortable with taking the falls from all the techniques.

Safety in training requires that the person taking the breakfalls be relaxed and confident in her ability to land safely. A poor falling partner not only is in danger of personal injury but also can cause injury to her partner as well.

SIDEFALL

The sidefall is performed by crossing one leg over the other to break your own balance (a), then falling to the side (b) and slapping the mat with your palm and forearm, thus absorbing the impact with your hand and arm rather than with your body (c). Note that the head is turned away from the fall with the chin tucked into the opposite shoulder to prevent a whiplash-type motion on impact.

To prevent injury, the slap must come at the exact moment that the shoulder hits the floor. If the arm hits before the body, you may break your arm because the body weight lands on the arm. If your arm makes contact after the body hits the floor, your shoulder will absorb the full impact of the fall. Last, but certainly not least, *do not land on your elbow!*

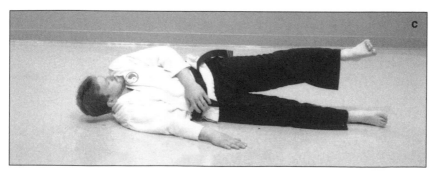

ROLLOUT

The rollout is designed to protect the student from a fall to the front, giving him an alternative to falling on his face. When propelled forward, the student reaches out, forming a circle with his arms (a), tucks his head, and allows himself to roll head over heels up his arm (b), across his back, and onto his feet (c).

Care must be taken once you enter the roll to pull the rear foot up underneath your body so that your feet are in the right position when you return to your feet. The feet should be in the same position when you land as when you started.

The rollout also allows you to cover a large distance quickly or vault over an object. You might need this skill in certain evasion situations, such as avoiding an oncoming car.

BACKFALL

When thrown onto your back, simply sit into the throw as if sitting into a chair (a), roll back onto your shoulders, and slap the mat with both hands to absorb the impact (b). The head must be tucked tightly into the collarbone at all times to prevent whiplash and to prevent cracking the head on the floor. The arms must be at a 45-degree angle to the body during impact.

During the early stages of practice, it is quite common to let the arms fly back and strike straight out from the shoulders. You must avoid this at all costs because the shoulders can be easily dislocated this way. Sometimes, even with the best attempt to control your fall, the force of the throw can take you into a complete roll. It makes no difference whether you roll the whole way over or not as long as you are not hurt in the fall and can return to your feet.

CHAPTER

6

PARRIES, BLOCKS, COUNTERSTRIKES, AND BREAKOUTS

The purpose of this chapter is to detail those specific skills necessary for a transition from traditional training-hall methodology to street combat. The purpose of these adaptations is to teach you how to work within the confines of a restricted area, for times when you are trapped and must defend against an attacker who is already too close for an escape or any big movements. Most Aikido systems instruct students to shorten up their motions if they do not have the proper amount of room, and this chapter illustrates the adaptations necessary to develop this ability.

FIGHTING STANCE

It is always preferable to position yourself in a stance that facilitates defensibility as well as ease and economy of motion. In the fighting stance, the defender stands sideways to the attacker with one hand (the lead hand) closer to the opponent and the other hand (the rear hand) farther away from the opponent. The lead hand should be held at waist level parallel to the floor, with the rear hand held at chin level to protect the face. The low lead is deceptive to the attacker, who sees it as a poor defense posture with a great opening to attack the face. In reality, this deception is the purpose of the stance. It draws the attack toward the face, thereby relieving you of having to worry about what part of the body to defend. Should the attack go toward the body, the lead hand is already in position to defend. The hands should always be open, not closed in fists, to enable you to sweep aside an attack rather than meeting force with force.

Place your body perpendicular to your opponent; you want to be in a full-side stance. Which foot and side to have closest to your opponent is up to you and how you feel most comfortable; just be aware that switching positions will reverse the prescribed method of executing the techniques that follow. For example, if an attacker throws a right cross and you want to perform a technique that sweeps his arm to the outside of his body, you could either do a lead-hand parry from a left-lead stance or a rear-hand parry from a right-lead stance.

Sixty percent of your weight should be on the lead foot. The rear heel should be raised ever so slightly off the floor, with the back leg tensed as a coiled spring ready to either pivot clear of an attack or help drive the hips and upper body into a counterstrike. This position helps to align the body to drive a strike. Any strike or counterstrike must use the entire body to give it power.

Many people are opposed to this stance because, with the weight forward, it is harder to retreat. Remember that the training philosophy for the street is that you have no room to retreat, which we explored in the section on standing your ground in chapter 4. Retreat may be a viable alternative if you have studied a hard style that dictates that you maneuver into a position to throw a big kick, but many trained martial artists have tripped over objects behind them or fallen off a curb into the street by trying to back up and launch a kick!

Fighting stance.

PARRIES

A parry is a slight deflecting motion of the arm or hand designed to redirect a strike (punch or kick). All parries, like breakouts, are done with the hand open and fingers extended. The palm should face the attacker for all punch defenses. As opposed to a hard block, which meets force with force and can drive the strike out away from the body, the parry merely causes the strike to miss its intended target while leaving the attacking arm well within range to trap and control. This type of redirection gives the assailant a false sense of security that his strike will land on target, and he may relax just a bit too much. If he encounters little resistance, and if the parry comes at the last possible second, he will be overly confident until it is too late.

Fencers and others adept at swordplay have long known the value of the parry in redirecting an attack. With a mere flick of the wrist, they can cause the best thrust to glance aside harmlessly while keeping their opponent within range for their own counterattack.

The lead-hand and rear-hand parries are illustrated on the following pages. The choice of which to use rests solely upon which technique you decide to initiate, based on your surroundings and preferences.

LEAD-HAND PARRY

The lead-hand parry is performed from the fighting stance. Tori sweeps his lead hand to the outside of his body, keeping the elbow tucked in tightly. Tori keeps his palm facing the attacker, and contact is made at the wrist, slightly deflecting the punch from its original target, tori's face. Tori tucks the thumb inside the hand to keep it out of the way.

REAR-HAND PARRY

The rear-hand parry is also performed from the fighting stance using the hand that is up under the chin. Tori uses a small circular motion to sweep the hand to the outside of the body, contacting the attacking arm at the wrist.

BLOCKS

Hard blocking is rarely used in Aikido, and only three blocks are ever used in a street situation: the double-bone block, the X-block, and the leg check. Blocking should be used instead of parrying when you are faced with a powerful attack such as a backfist or a roundhouse kick. These attacks are arching motions that come in from the side rather than from straight in. As such, they gain tremendous power and momentum from the extended body motion during delivery. If you cannot evade such an attack or redirect it with a parry, then you should use a hard block to stop it.

DOUBLE-BONE BLOCK

The outside double-bone block is used primarily against a high roundhouse kick, but it may also be used against a backfist, as shown here. This type of block can be very punishing to practice over and over but is much safer against a strike as powerful as a backfist. A block using only the outside of the arm can result in a broken arm.

Tori executes the block by sweeping the arm upward, keeping the upper arm parallel to the floor. At the height of the arc, tori clenches his hand in a fist and turns his wrist so that the back of his hand faces the oncoming strike. Tori deflects the strike with the forearm.

X-BLOCK

The X-block is a hard block using crossed arms to stop an attack when you are not in position to defend against it otherwise.

The X-block is always used in conjunction with a slight step to the rear. This may seem like a minor detail, especially if you have trained in a martial art that teaches you to pull your punches in practice. But remember that you should train for contact at all times to avoid getting used to dealing with anything other than a real strike. If your training partner or attacker is committed to driving her punch for maximum effect, which is several inches through your body, imagine what would happen to her fist if it were merely deflected downward with the X-block. Her body strike has now turned into an excellent groin strike! In stepping back, you are removing her intended target while you redirect her strike into position for your own lock.

Shown here is the X-block being used against a low punch to the body; it is also used against a reverse punch to the body. As tori steps to the rear, both hands (closed in fists) are drawn up slightly to just above the waist, then brought down sharply against the attacking limb with one hand crossing over the other to form an X. The attack is met at the wrists where the arms are crossed.

LEG CHECK

The third type of block is the leg check, which is also illustrated in chapter 10 on combination defenses. It is designed to absorb the impact of a low roundhouse kick aimed at the knee. When tori is attacked in this fashion, he raises the knee of the lead leg, bringing the thigh parallel to the floor and the foot up as far as possible. By using this technique, the impact of the kick is taken on the outer calf, effectively smothering the kick. It is important to note that tori's balance should not be compromised at this point. The weight should remain centered and *not* transferred entirely to the rear foot.

COUNTERSTRIKES

Counterstrikes are used to help end a confrontation. Their purpose is to stop uke's attack midstream and set up your own technique. Students should pull these defensive strikes short of contact when practicing but remember to throw all offensive (attacking) strikes for full contact so the defender becomes accustomed to dealing with real strikes.

Aikidoka are not totally without offensive weapons. Nor should they be afraid to make use of what is available. The one thing that distinguishes self-defense–oriented Aikido styles is their use of the "stop hit" (teishi suru) or "defensive preparatory strike." The purpose of this is to either knock out your opponent or daze him enough to escape or take further defensive action. As we discussed earlier in this text, we are assuming that the student has been trapped or closed in and has no way of escape except through the attacker. Traditional Aikidoka call this "atemi." Although most schools advocate use of atemi, few teach its application as part of each technique.

The stop hit takes several different forms depending on the means of attack, including, but not limited to, the lead punch, rear cross, reverse punch, and the groin kick.

LEAD PUNCH

Popularized by Bruce Lee, this strike is extremely powerful, as are most straight punches. It is performed from a fighting stance and is thrown as a counterstrike while parrying the opponent's strike. It is used to cut off the attacker's assault and daze him long enough to set up your technique. This strike is being adopted by more and more martial artists and street fighters and is usually thrown as an offensive strike from a stance putting the strong side of the body forward. For a right-handed person, this would mean standing with the right hand forward in a left-handed stance. (Note that a right-handed stance has the left hand and foot forward; the left-handed stance has the right hand and foot forward. In martial arts and boxing, generally the weaker hand is held in front to block while the stronger hand is held in the rear to strike.) It works equally well as a stop hit from a normal (left-lead, right-handed) stance. Targets for the lead punch include the face and the body.

To execute the lead punch, start with the striking arm at the low lead position and punch straight to the target.

REAR CROSS

The rear cross is one of the most powerful strikes in any fighter's arsenal. Its power comes from a slight rotation of the hips as it is thrown. The rear hand, which is held under the chin, travels straight to its target, while the lead hand comes up to the chin for protection. Its effectiveness comes from the ability to make it "come out of nowhere." This strike requires no windup and is very easy to throw without "telegraphing," which means to tip off the attacker by using a big windup before throwing the punch. The body and hips must be rotated to deliver the power that would be generated with a big windup. The target of this strike is just above the chin where the lip connects. This area of the chin is a major nerve center for the head, and a well-placed blow can easily deliver a quick knockout.

At no time should this strike be delivered to the nose. The force of this strike could drive the bone in the nose into the brain, causing permanent brain damage or even death. If the attacker is measurably taller than you are, the alternate target can be the sternum, which will knock the wind out of the lungs, temporarily incapacitating him. If you are on your knees or are seated, the target area becomes the groin. In short, strike the most vulnerable area within reach.

REVERSE PUNCH

The reverse punch is executed in a similar manner to the rear cross, except that it travels up from the hip rather than in a straight line. Your hand is turned over so that the clenched fingers are toward the ground. This gives a slight rotating motion to the hand as the punch is delivered and gives it extra power. The same safety precautions and target areas mentioned for the rear cross apply to the reverse punch.

It is important to note here that this is used primarily when defending against a wrist grab. This strike will travel from the hip upward while the other hand is brought up in a sweeping circular motion to the "breakout" position (see pages 78, 83-87). Note also that you must be facing the attacker when throwing a reverse punch and therefore not in a fighting stance.

The reverse punch is typically seen in Karate, usually beginning with the lead hand extended and the rear hand turned palm upward at the hip. As the rear hand is thrown, the lead hand is usually, but not always, pulled back to the hip to give power through the opposing motion. The strike is delivered with the fist turned palm downward. I have modified this slightly for Aikido in that the rear hand is swept up in front of the body to facilitate the breakout rather than being drawn back to the hip.

GROIN KICK

The groin kick is fairly self-explanatory in terms of its effect on your opponent, but the technique described here is done just a little differently from that in other systems or arts. Instead of aiming your kicks with your toes, I recommend using the entire top surface of the foot as a punter does in football.

The rationale for using the top surface of the foot is that if you are indeed trapped, your attacker is too close for you to get off a good kick. So you should learn to get the kick in with whatever part of the foot or shin happens to be within range. If you are too close, the shin will still make contact. If you are too far away, the pointing of the toes will help you get that little extra bit of reach. Most toe kicks will miss their target if the opponent moves even the least bit. Likewise, kicks using the ball of the foot are also ineffective if the groin is the target.

The main complaint about hitting the target with the toes is that it can severely strain your foot. What must be considered here is the very soft, delicate nature of the tissue this kick is intended to strike. The kick is not aimed with the toes, but they offer a little extra reach if necessary.

When performing this kick, tori draws the knee up until the thigh is parallel to the floor; the toes are pointed and then snapped upward, extending the leg straight toward its target.

BREAKOUT-COUNTERSTRIKE COMBINATIONS

The term "breakout" is actually a misnomer because rarely does the student ever really break completely free of her attacker. The breakout motion is actually a method of breaking the strength of the assailant's grip. By letting your opponent keep a partial grip on you, you keep his limbs within range to trap, control, lock, break, throw, or use any combination thereof.

The counterstrikes that follow the breakout techniques consist of stop hits and kicks that are used to either disable the attacker or daze him long enough to perform some other controlling technique.

WRIST-GRAB ATTACKS

Wrist grabs are a reality in any given defense situation. They may be initiated as a means of attack themselves but most often are the result of a "trap." Trapping is used to control the opponent in many martial-arts systems. It results from your attacker blocking your arm as you strike or counterstrike and grabbing the wrist to try to control you. Once you have learned to escape from the static wrist grabs, you will be well prepared to respond if you wind up in one of these grips during a confrontation.

The most common grips you will encounter are illustrated on the following pages. Each grip does not have a different breakout technique. The defensive techniques when attacked with grips #1, #2, and #5 are usually identical. Likewise, execution of any given technique is exactly the same when faced with grips #3 or #4.

GRIP #1 (KATATE-TORI)

A single-hand grab to the same-side wrist of the other person.

GRIP #2 (GYAKU-KATATE-TORI)

A reversed single-hand grab to the same-side wrist of the other person.

GRIP #3 (DOSOKYU-KATATE-TORI)

A single-hand cross-body wrist grab.

GRIP #4 (RYOTE-IPPO-TORI)

A two-hand cross-body wrist grab.

GRIP #5 (MAE-RYOTE-TORI)

A straight two-hand wrist grab.

GRIP #6 (USHIRO-KATATE-TORI)

A straight two-hand wrist grab from the rear.

GRIP #7 (USHIRO-TORI)

A traditional bear hug.

It is extremely important to keep the hand open and the fingers extended when executing a breakout. Many people attempt to perform this motion with a closed fist and wonder why it seems so difficult.

By simply extending the fingers as if reaching for something just out of your grasp, all the muscles in the arm are brought into play, not just the biceps, making it very easy to escape from the strongest grip. A simple demonstration of this power is in the "Aikido unbendable arm."

Face your partner and rest your arm at the wrist on his shoulder while making a fist (thumb pointed upward). He then places both hands on your arm at the elbow and presses down. Try as you might, you will never be able to keep your arm straight.

Now try the same test again, this time extending your fingers as if reaching for the wall behind him, and relax. He will turn 12 shades of purple trying to bend your arm as you relax and look as if you are not even trying. Although this exercise is widely used to demonstrate the power of ki, it is simple body physiology. By extending the fingers, you are firing the neurons to every muscle fiber in your arm. By making a fist, you focus your body's energy into the biceps alone—a lesson to remember throughout your training.

BREAKOUT AND REVERSE PUNCH

This maneuver, used to escape grips #1, #2, and #5, is executed as follows: Tori sweeps his grabbed hand upward with his palm turned toward his face. Shown here against grip #1, tori sweeps the hand in a circular motion until the fingers point toward the ceiling, keeping the elbow tucked in against the body. At the same time, tori throws a reverse punch to uke's chin with his free hand.

REVERSE BOWSTRING DRAW
AND REVERSE PUNCH

This technique is effective against grips #1, #2, and #5. Grip #1 is
shown here. In this case, tori pulls the grabbed hand back
alongside the face with the palm turned outward. As tori draws
the hand back, he delivers a reverse punch with his free hand.

Once again, keep the hand open and turn it so the palm is facing
outward away from the face. This will never work if tori's fist is
clenched. It will merely turn into a power struggle or wrestling
match. As the hand is drawn toward tori, uke is actually being
pulled into tori's punch, doubling his striking power.

SIDE BREAKOUT AND REVERSE PUNCH

This combination is also a defense against grips #1, #2, and #5. Grip #1 is shown here. Tori takes a deep step to the right while extending his arm at a 45-degree angle toward the floor, breaking uke's balance while simultaneously executing a reverse punch to the chin. Tori extends the fingers once more as he goes out to the side for maximum effect on uke's balance.

CIRCULAR BREAKOUT AND GROIN KICK

Used in defense of grips #3 and #4. Grip #3 is shown here. Tori breaks out of uke's grip by executing an open-handed, clockwise, circular motion with the arm almost fully extended and grasps uke's arm at 12 o'clock. As tori's hand reaches 12 o'clock, he executes a front-snap kick to the groin.

LIFT AND GROIN KICK

Use this technique only against grips #3 and #4. Grip #4 is shown here. Tori cradles uke's attacking hand with his palm toward his face and lifts it straight up to eye level while performing a front-snap kick to the groin, making sure to point the toe as a punter would.

At no time should the attacker's wrist be grabbed; it should be cradled. Cradling the hand involves keeping tori's palm turned toward his face, keeping his fingers extended, and letting uke's wrist ride on the web between tori's forefinger and thumb. If tori grabs the wrist, it will reduce his ability to lift the arm.

CHAPTER

7

WRIST
TECHNIQUES

With this chapter, I begin detailing the actual application of techniques. I want to suggest that you keep your place marked to chapter 4 for references to posture, picking the landing site, standing your ground, redirecting your opponent, breaking the balance, pressure-point manipulation, counterstriking, and softening blows. All the techniques in the following chapters will make references to these principles, and it is imperative for proper learning that you refer to these sections frequently.

All the techniques you learn should eventually be practiced with both hands in order to cover *any* possibility. It is necessary, though, to thoroughly master the technique one way first, then reverse it. If you try to practice with both hands at the beginning, you will become confused. To perform any of the techniques shown here on your nondominant side, simply practice being attacked with the other hand, and perform all your motions and steps with the nondominant hands and feet.

Throughout the book, you may notice that very little is mentioned regarding footwork or placement. To adapt to the street, you must assume that you have no room to maneuver and that you will be forced to drop all the big footwork to be able to perform the techniques when trapped. If small amounts of footwork are necessary for any of the techniques, the text will describe them.

I have arranged the techniques and the variations in the manner in which they are taught to most Aikido students in most schools. I cannot stress strongly enough that there is no right or wrong technique to use in any given situation or against a given attacker. The difference in this type of training is that there is no set response to a certain grab or strike. Each technique is taught to apply to all variations of attack to give you a much wider repertoire on which to draw. In the following chapters, you will see many possible wrist, arm, and body techniques that can be used against the same strikes, kicks, and grips. The technique you choose is determined by your surroundings and circumstances and by what you feel works best for you. Many techniques and thousands more possible variations exist. It is my hope that this book will provide you with some of the basics and help you discover some things you may have never before considered.

This chapter focuses on joint locks to the wrist. Although the arm is sometimes locked at the elbow at the same time, the control of the attacker's arm is at the wrist joint, not the elbow. Some techniques end in a throw after the lock and some do not, depending on the position in which the lock is achieved.

KOTE-GAESHI

Kote-gaeshi is a wrist lock in which the attacker's wrist is turned outward and to the side away from his body. Because of the structure of the wrist, it becomes locked after turning approximately 45 degrees. The result is that the opponent is thrown to the ground to avoid fracturing the wrist or forearm. This technique does not rely on strength. Only proper application of technique will result in a good, forceful throw.

It is of the utmost importance for this technique that you remember the principles of posture and picking the landing site. To ensure that you have proper control, always keep your hips under your shoulders. Never bend over at the waist when executing this throw; instead, bend your knees and drop your weight down. In picking the landing site, remember that the attacker will attempt to protect himself in this fall, if he can, by falling where he wants to go. Maintain control of the wrist at all times, bringing the hand down to your knee so he will drop straight down into a harder fall.

A common error students make in the body-punch defense variation is to grab up too high on the attacker's wrist. By this I mean grabbing too close to the base of the hand. You must keep at least a thumb's width between your hand and the base of the attacker's hand. If you grab too high, your hand is actually supporting the wrist that you are trying to bend.

It is also very important that uke's hand be held close to your chest. If you try to make the throw work by pushing the hand out away from your body, you lose pressure and will end up off-balance on the throw. The power in this technique is in the force of your body weight being applied to the joint. This power can be focused in an area as little as a fingertip placed against the back of the hand.

TECHNIQUE TIPS—KOTE-GAESHI

1. Keep your hands together on this lock.
2. Turn uke's palm down toward the floor as you turn it out.
3. Keep your hands at waist level for better leverage.
4. Keep your back straight with upright posture during the throw; don't bend over.
5. Maintain your grip on uke's hand after the throw.

KOTE-GAESHI BODY-PUNCH DEFENSE

The body-punch defense is performed from a normal stance facing the attacker, not from a fighting stance.

Against a right-handed body punch, tori takes a step back with her right foot and performs an X-block with the left hand on top (a). Grasping uke's outstretched arm at the wrist with the left hand, tori caps the hand in the same way she does for the face punch (b), steps out at a 45-degree angle with the right foot, keeping uke's hand in front of her body, and applies downward pressure on the hand (c), throwing him to the ground.

KOTE-GAESHI GRIP #6 DEFENSE

This time uke attacks from the rear, grabbing both of tori's arms at the wrists. From this attack, tori takes a slight step back with her right foot as she executes a right elbow strike to her attacker's ribs (a). This is nothing more than bringing the elbow back sharply into uke's ribs, thus making him release his grip on the wrist. If the grip causes uke to release both hands, run away. Tori then pivots 180 degrees and grabs the wrist with her free (right) hand (b) and completes the kote-gaeshi grip (c). Turning the hand out to the side at a 45-degree angle, tori throws uke to the ground (d).

The grip here is the primary concern in making this technique work. Your thumbs should be pointed up the back of the hand and held together, touching at both knuckles. Your fingers should be curled around into the palm. Grip uke's hand so it flattens out in your grasp. Many beginning students attempt to press on the back of the hand with the tips of

their thumbs, thus losing a great deal of strength in the grip.

In addition, without the use of a final pivot as taught in the dojo, hand placement in a street combat situation is very important. Uke's hand should be turned out at a 45-degree angle and brought down to the side of tori's knee. Bending slightly at the knees to keep the back straight will direct his fall almost straight down, adding a harder fall to the joint lock. An additional benefit here is that by dropping uke where he stands, tori is in position to control with further locks if needed. To do this, however, tori *must* maintain her grip on the hand even after the throw is completed.

Once again, as with the body-punch defense, keep your hands close to your body. For this variation, keep your hands at waist level and apply pressure with your wrist. Do not push uke's wrist out away from your body in an attempt to direct him.

SHIHO-NAGE

Shiho-nage is very much a wrist throw, but it relies mostly on the student using his body weight to move the attacker. At no time when practicing this technique should undue torque be put on the arm, and brute strength should not be used. The attacker should feel as light as a feather when this is executed properly. This, takes some practice, so don't be discouraged if it does not come naturally the first few times you execute this technique.

In performing this technique, the attacker's attacking arm is swept across his body, forcing him to pivot 180 degrees as you continue your motion to also pivot 180 degrees. The resulting position has the attacker and you in a mutual "elbow-to-shoulder" position facing away from each other.

This ending position is very important. You end in a horse-stance with the knees bent and back straight, as if seated on a horse. The elbow of the controlling arm should be making contact with the attacker's shoulder. Likewise, the attacker's elbow should be resting on the back of your shoulder.

When performing the throw, your arm is brought down in a motion similar to swinging a hammer while you step out into a "lunge." At no time should the arm be pulled out from the body. If the throw is to be effective, proper contact must be maintained on the arm. If the contact is lost, the control of the throw is lost. It is also possible for you to severely injure your training partner by wrenching the arm at the shoulder. You must let go of the attacker's arm when your throwing arm gets parallel to the floor. Trying to hold on to the arm too long will result in a sloppy and dangerous throw for your partner.

This can be a very gentle technique or a very vicious throw depending on the amount of torque used on the throw.

It is absolutely imperative in both of the following variations to coordinate the hand and foot movements during your pivot, as if the two were tied together. In this way, the attacker seems almost weightless. If this is not done, it will be extremely difficult to move him because you really have no leverage from this position to use upper-body strength.

TECHNIQUE TIPS—SHIHO-NAGE

1. Never sweep in a flat line; maintain your circle.
2. Step at the same time you sweep with your hand.
3. End your pivot in a horse-stance to maintain your balance.
4. Lunge out, stepping with the same side foot as the arm you are throwing with.
5. Keep your body upright and don't bend over during the throw.

SHIHO-NAGE GRIP #1 DEFENSE

Uke attacks with grip #1. Tori responds with a breakout and reverse punch to the chin (a). Tori now reaches across with her left hand and grasps uke's wrist, making sure that her thumb is positioned on the inside of uke's wrist. She then begins to sweep the hand in a downward arc until it reaches approximately 6 o'clock (b). When the hand reaches this position, tori must begin to move her right foot in one coordinated motion with her left hand as she executes a 180-degree pivot ending in a horse-stance (c) with uke's arm locked up at the shoulder. Step-

ping forward with her left foot, tori pulls down on the attacker's arm (d), breaking his balance to the rear and throwing him onto his back.

SHIHO-NAGE GRIP #1 DEFENSE
(CONTINUED)

SHIHO-NAGE CLUB-STRIKE DEFENSE

A lead-hand parry is used against a downward club strike to the head (a), followed by a rear cross to the chin. Tori then sweeps the hand in an outward circle and controls it with her right hand (b). Cross stepping to the right with her left foot (c), tori pivots 180 degrees into position for the throw (d).

SHIHO-NAGE CLUB-STRIKE DEFENSE
(CONTINUED)

YUKI-CHIGAI (SANKYO)

Yuki-chigai is a wrist-locking and throwing technique designed to either control a foe with extreme pain or break the attacker's arm and throw him to the ground. The attacker's arm ends in a box-shaped position with the wrist, elbow, and shoulder joints locked.

This technique must be practiced with great care because it is extremely dangerous. You can easily break your training partner's arm or dislocate his shoulder if you are not careful. It is also very important that your partner never resist your attempts to employ this lock. To do so adds twice as much torque to the arms and your partner can actually break his own arm in the process.

When attempting to throw from this technique, it is very important to remember your posture and step forward in a lunging motion with your back straight. Do not bend forward on this throw. When practicing, your partner may tell you he feels no real compulsion to go along with your throw, but if uke's arm had been broken from the lock, he would be more than willing to cooperate with you.

TECHNIQUE TIPS—YUKI-CHIGAI

1. Do not let uke's wrist turn within your grasp.
2. Keep uke's arm in a box-shaped lock with the arm perpendicular to the floor.
3. Maintain your position beside uke when employing this lock.
4. Do not let uke turn away from the lock and escape.
5. Practice this technique with great care.

YUKI-CHIGAI GRIP #1 DEFENSE

Tori is attacked with grip #1. In response, she executes a side breakout. Tori steps sharply to the side, delivering a reverse punch to the chin (a). With her opponent now dazed and off-balance, tori steps through with her left foot and pivots 180 degrees underneath uke's outstretched arm (b). As she turns to complete the pivot, tori will remove her right hand from uke's grip and grasp the attacking hand in an overhand grip (c). She completes the pivot, ending up beside uke with her feet in the same line as her assailant. Tori brings uke's arm into a box-shaped lock, turning his hand inward and upward, achieving a painful joint lock (d). From this position, tori can step forward with her right foot, pulling straight out on uke's arm, thus breaking his balance to the front and flipping the attacker over onto his back (e).

YUKI-CHIGAI FACE-PUNCH DEFENSE

Tori executes a rear-hand parry against uke's right-face punch
(a). Uke's arm is swept to the inside and fed into tori's waiting left
hand (b). Tori then steps in with her right foot (c), pivots into
position for the lock (d), and finishes with a throw.

KOTE-KUDAKI

This technique epitomizes the essence of Aikido. It uses practically no force, and, in most variations, only one finger is used to apply the pressure. The balance is broken by means of a softening blow or counterstrike to set this technique up. This is a wrist technique designed to at least cause extreme pain, bringing the hapless attacker to his knees or, if need be, break the arm and stop the attack. Be very careful with this one; it hits a lot faster than you might think. No strength is involved in the performance of this move. In fact, should the user try to use brute force, the technique becomes only marginally effective and can actually turn into a wrestling match with the opponent.

This technique also employs locks to more than one joint on the arm, but the primary force is focused on the wrist. Pressure can be directed to the wrist or the elbow, depending on the variation.

TECHNIQUE TIPS—KOTE-KUDAKI

1. Turn uke's hand completely over so the back of his hand is on your chest.
2. Remember to hold uke's hand firmly against your body.
3. Keep your arm and hand relaxed and loose.
4. Move your hand in a question-mark motion.
5. Bend your knees slightly as you take uke down.

KOTE-KUDAKI GRIP #3 DEFENSE

When defending against grip #3 (a), tori places her left hand on top of uke's to hold it in place (b), making sure to turn her thumb toward herself as if she were going to apply the kote-gaeshi grip, then makes a clockwise circular motion. As tori's hand nears the top of the arc, she turns her palm toward uke's body, using the edge of her hand as a knife blade (c). As tori continues the circle, uke's wrist is trapped and locked (d), forcing him to the floor to escape the pressure of the lock and prevent breaking the arm.

KOTE-KUDAKI GRIP #3 DEFENSE
(CONTINUED)

c

d

KOTE-KUDAKI BODY-PUNCH DEFENSE

Against a body punch, tori takes a step backward and uses the X-block illustrated earlier in this text (a). Once the strike has been deflected, tori secures uke's wrist by grabbing with the top hand (b), and then turns the hand completely over so the back of uke's hand is lying flat upon tori's upper chest around the collarbone area (c). With the armbar (straight-arm lock) in place, tori hooks the inside of uke's arm at the elbow joint with the little finger of her right hand, then exerts downward pressure on uke's arm at the elbow, bringing him to his knees in pain (d).

KOTE-KUDAKI BODY-PUNCH DEFENSE
(CONTINUED)

CHAPTER

8

ARM
TECHNIQUES

rm techniques differ from wrist techniques in where the pressure is applied. Most arm techniques involve either a controlling armbar or an elbow-breaking maneuver designed for life-threatening situations. Great care should be taken not to actually strike the elbow when practicing these techniques; the elbow joint is very fragile and can easily be damaged.

Arm techniques apply pressure to the elbow joint using either direct pressure just above the elbow after applying an armbar or a strike to the same area in a life-threatening situation. Either way these techniques can be quite debilitating.

ROBUSE (IKKYO)

Robuse is an elbow-smashing technique to be used only when your life is in danger and when a lesser option is out of the question. This technique will probably cause permanent loss of function of the attacker's arm, and I cannot stress strongly enough that it be used only against a weapon attack or to protect your life.

The balance is broken by means of softening blows and redirection of the attacker. Pay strict attention to your balance and posture while executing. Your knees should be bent and your upper body should be as erect as possible. Your weight should be evenly distributed between both feet. While uke's arm is fully extended, deliver a strike to the elbow joint to break the arm, using your knee as a platform for the break.

TECHNIQUE TIPS—ROBUSE

1. Keep your thumb in the web of uke's hand (except in grip #3 or grip #4 defense).
2. Remember to sweep the arm in a circular motion, breaking uke's balance upward.
3. Do not lose or relax your grip on uke's hand.
4. Hold uke's hand firmly against your knee.
5. Deliver your strike to the back of uke's arm, just above the elbow.

ROBUSE FACE-PUNCH DEFENSE

Uke attacks with a left-lead punch and is met with a rear-hand parry and a lead-punch cross to the chin (a). Grabbing the back of the hand (b), tori steps back, pulling uke's hand back and down in a circular sweep into a straight armbar to set it up for a strike with the palm and break (c).

ROBUSE GRIP #2 DEFENSE

Tori will use the reverse bowstring draw breakout if grabbed in grip #2 (a). Tori pulls his right hand back as if drawing a bow and turns it over at the last minute so his palm faces toward the floor. Tori simultaneously delivers a reverse punch to the chin (b). With uke now disoriented, tori reaches across his face and secures uke's outstretched hand with his own left hand; tori sweeps uke's hand in an upward arc across his body (c) as he steps out to his side and brings the hand down to his bent knee. He then turns his hips and shoulders 90 degrees and brings his fist down onto the elbow, breaking the arm (d).

ROBUSE GRIP #4 DEFENSE

For grip #4 (a), tori will execute the circular breakout and groin kick (b). At the top of the circle (12 o'clock), tori turns his hand over and grabs uke's wrist (c). Then, stepping to the rear with his right foot and pulling uke's hand in an arcing sweep to his own knee, tori ends with a strike to uke's elbow, breaking the arm (d).

UDE-HISHIGI

Ude-hishigi is an elbow-breaking technique that can be used to cause a convincing amount of pain. This technique can control the attacker or completely break the arm if it is necessary. Ude-hishigi will probably cause permanent loss of function to the attacker's arm if used full force and should be used full force only against a potentially lethal attack.

Ude-hishigi uses softening blows and redirection to set up the technique. Pay particular attention to your posture on this one, and keep your back straight. This technique employs a straight armbar and can be used to control your attacker with pain or break his arm, if necessary.

TECHNIQUE TIPS—UDE-HISHIGI

1. Keep your thumb in the web of uke's hand (except in grip #3 or grip #4 defense).
2. Remember to sweep uke's arm in a circular motion, breaking his balance upward.
3. Do not lose or relax your grip on uke's hand.
4. Hold uke's hand firmly against your chest.
5. Apply pressure just above the elbow joint with your elbow.
6. Apply pressure gently in practice for your partner's safety.

UDE-HISHIGI GRIP #5 DEFENSE

As illustrated here, tori will use the reverse bowstring draw breakout if grabbed in grip #5 (a). Tori pulls his right hand back as if drawing a bow then turns his palm away from his face. Tori delivers a reverse punch to the chin at the same time he performs the breakout (b). With uke now disoriented, tori reaches across his face and secures the back of uke's outstretched hand (c). Tori then steps back and pivots 90 degrees, pulling uke's hand up to his collarbone with his arm across his body, and positions his own arm on top to position it for the break. As tori exerts pressure just above uke's elbow with his own elbow, he bends his knees slightly, applying an extremely painful armbar (d).

UDE-HISHIGI GRIP #5 DEFENSE
(CONTINUED)

UDE-HISHIGI GRIP #7 DEFENSE

Grabbed from behind in an attempted bear hug, tori spots the hands coming around with his peripheral (side) vision and raises his elbows abruptly out from his sides (a). Simultaneously, tori performs an elbow strike with his right elbow into uke's solar plexus (b) and grabs uke's left wrist. Sliding out under the left arm, tori takes a position beside the attacker, with uke's arm extended into a straight armbar with the hand held tightly against tori's sternum (c). Placing the elbow of his right arm onto uke's arm just above the elbow, tori applies pressure and either controls the arm with a painful lock or breaks the elbow joint (d).

UDE-HISHIGI GRIP #7 DEFENSE
(CONTINUED)

CHAPTER

9

BODY TECHNIQUES

Body techniques use the attacker's broken balance to set up a throw. They do not use strictly a joint lock or armbar but rather pressure applied to certain parts of the body after breaking the attacker's balance. This can be done in many different ways. Once you deliver the initial strike, your attacker's balance may well be completely broken. If not, other methods are just as useful now that your attacker is at least dazed. You can sweep the arm across the body to turn the attacker into a twisted position; apply pressure to any number of tender pressure points around the head, neck, and facial area; or simply apply direct pressure against one shoulder, putting all your attacker's weight on one foot, then sweep that foot out from under him.

MUKAE-DAOSHI

Mukae-daoshi is a potentially devastating body throw in which the attacker is thrown straight backward onto his back and shoulders. Like so many other throws, you have the option of making this a fairly easy throw by applying gentle pressure, or a full-force throw by striking the face and spine. This technique uses a distinct scissors motion of the arms forcing backward on the attacker's head while pressing in on the base of the spine. This movement causes the attacking person to take a fall similar to falling backward over a fence or other waist-high object.

Although the neck is locked out on this technique, it is not a neck-breaking move. The sweep of the arms must be synchronized to get the opposing motion necessary to knock the attacker's lower body out from under him and make him fall on his upper back, shoulders, and neck.

TECHNIQUE TIPS—MUKAE-DAOSHI

1. Sweep uke's hand in a downward circular sweep.
2. Turn uke only 90 degrees.
3. Place your forearm against uke's upper lip just below the nose; roll your upper arm into and across the nose to break uke's balance.
4. Place your other hand in the small of uke's back and maintain pressure.

MUKAE-DAOSHI GRIP #1 DEFENSE

Uke attacks with grip #1. Tori uses the breakout and reverse punch (a) to loosen his grip and daze or knock uke out. With uke now a little more cooperative, tori reaches across the body to grasp his foe's left wrist (b) with the thumb on the inside of the wrist. Tori will now sweep the hand in a downward arc back across the body (see "Redirecting Your Opponent" in chapter 4), twisting uke's wrist and causing him to turn 90 degrees (c). Uke should now be in a position with his left side facing tori and poised up on his toes with his balance tipped to the rear. At this point, tori will simultaneously strike uke's mouth area with the upper forearm, rolling it up into his nose while striking the small of the back (d) with the thumb side of his right hand (fingers should be extended with thumb tucked inside the hand and palm facing the floor), forcing him into a backfall (e).

MUKAE-DAOSHI GRIP #1 DEFENSE
(CONTINUED)

MUKAE-DAOSHI FACE-PUNCH DEFENSE

When attacked with a lead-hand face punch, tori uses a rear-hand parry simultaneously with a lead punch (a). Uke's outstretched hand is then swept in a circular motion to the outside of the body down into tori's waiting left hand (b) and swept upward until uke is off-balance (c). Finally, tori strikes uke's face and back in the scissors motion (d), which takes uke into a backfall.

ASHI-WAZA

An extremely effective body throw, ashi-waza employs hip rotation as its main force to take the aggressor off-balance and throw him. (See "Breaking the Balance" in chapter 4.)

No amount of pulling with arm strength will make this throw effective. Your arms must be locked into position once the opponent is grabbed and held in place throughout your pivot.

Ashi-waza is especially designed to handle the roundhouse or "cowboy" punch. The simplicity of the application is the real beauty of this motion. It is designed for use against a full-force punch in which uke's momentum is carrying him toward you. By sidestepping the attack and pulling uke farther in the direction he is already moving, his balance is broken, which leads to a spectacular throw.

Some systems employ a trip with this technique where tori blocks the ankle of uke's front foot with his (tori's) foot. But this is usually not necessary because the force of pulling uke's sleeve or arm to the outside of his body is sufficient to break his balance.

TECHNIQUE TIPS—ASHI-WAZA

1. Step into the attack.
2. Use your grip on the sleeve or upper arm for leverage.
3. Pull down and away from your body to lead uke into the throw.

ASHI-WAZA FACE-PUNCH DEFENSE

When uke attacks with a big roundhouse punch (a), tori merely turns at the waist and hooks uke's arm just above the elbow, grabbing the sleeve or the flesh at the back of the upper arm (b). Tori places his right hand on uke's neck as uke is slightly pulled in the direction he already wanted to go (c), leading him into a hard fall.

ASHI-WAZA ADAPTATIONS

The following adaptations are similar to ashi-waza in that they require tori to grab and control uke's sleeve or upper arm and pull it to tori's side and downward while attacking a pressure point, causing uke to throw himself because of his lost balance. If a pressure point is used, uke will lose his balance as he tries to escape the pain. Tori can also apply direct pressure to uke's upper body, forcing him off balance; and then, with a sharp tug on the sleeve, throw him to the ground. The same can be done by sweeping uke's leg out from under him after his balance is broken.

SHOMEN-ATE

Shomen-ate is similar to ashi-waza in that it is applied by controlling the attacking arm at the sleeve. This time uke's head is swept back by applying force under the chin with tori's other hand.

TSUME-OTOSHI

Similar to ashi-waza in that the sleeve is controlled, tsume-otoshi requires that tori break uke's balance by applying a pressure-point attack. Tori grabs the collarbone with the fingers, just as an eagle grabs with talons.

KUBI-WAZA

In the kubi-waza technique, pressure is applied to uke's neck on a pressure point under the jawbone with one finger pressing upward. As he rears back to escape the pressure, his balance is broken, facilitating the take-down.

O-SOTO-GARI

In the o-soto-gari technique, tori grabs uke's shirt at the sleeve and the opposing shoulder as he steps to the side, pulling uke onto one foot. The leg is then swept out from under uke.

DO-GAESHI

Do-gaeshi is another body throw that also requires no physical strength to perform. The secret to all these techniques is proper execution and body motion, not brute strength. A fairly simple technique, do-gaeshi is performed at the beginning in much the same way as the mukae-daoshi. You must maintain a straight back and upright position throughout your motion.

Uke is turned 90 degrees and his balance is broken to the rear by the sweep on the arm that has turned him into this position. Once he is in this position, tori extends his arm across uke's throat and sweeps his arms to the rear, taking uke into a fall.

TECHNIQUE TIPS—DO-GAESHI

1. Sweep uke's hand in a downward circular sweep.
2. Turn uke only 90 degrees.
3. Sweep your arm across uke's throat, breaking his balance to the rear.
4. Turn at the waist, keeping your arm stiff, to throw uke to the rear.
5. Return to a fighting stance after the throw, keeping your eyes on uke at all times.

DO-GAESHI GRIP #4 DEFENSE

Uke grabs tori with grip #4 (a). Tori responds with the lift-and-groin-kick break-out (b). Without first putting his foot down in its original position, tori uses his body weight to shift and step straight back into a 90-degree pivot while sweeping uke's arm in a downward circular motion and pulls uke's throat up his straight arm (c) into position for the throw. Tori turns at the hip 90 degrees and throws uke to the side over his leg (d).

DO-GAESHI FACE-PUNCH DEFENSE

For a lead-hand punch, tori uses a rear-hand parry and a lead punch (a). Tori then grabs uke's left wrist with his own left hand, controlling it and sweeping it down to waist level (b). Stepping into his attacker, tori extends his right arm across uke's throat (c), breaking his balance to the rear for the throw (d).

DO-GAESHI ADAPTATIONS

The following techniques are derived from my own Aikido system, Tejitsu, and are used as alternatives to those previously illustrated. The initial technique setup is identical to do-gaeshi.

HANA-NAGE

Once uke is off-balance, tori simply hooks the nose with two fingers and, with a stroking motion similar to petting a dog's head, sweeps him backward into a throw.

GYAKU-ATE

Here tori's hand is turned over and hooked under the attacker's chin, and he is swept backward.

KAITEN-NAGE

Kaiten-nage is often called a "wheel throw" because the attacker is flipped forward into either a forward roll or a flip onto the back. This is a particularly effective technique because few opponents know how to gracefully roll out of this type of throw, and most will land very hard, doing a midair flip onto the back.

This throw is executed by applying pressure forward and downward against uke's head while forcing his arms up behind him. This forces uke into a forward roll, if he knows how to do it. By applying a little more pressure to the head and arm, he will flip forward in mid-air and land on his back.

TECHNIQUE TIPS—KAITEN-NAGE

1. Maintain a firm grip on uke's hand as you raise it behind his back.
2. Continue upward pressure on uke's arm as you force the head down.
3. In practice, let uke roll out of this technique and avoid flipping him in midair.

KAITEN-NAGE FACE-PUNCH DEFENSE

Uke's punching attack is deflected with a rear-hand parry (a). The outstretched hand is then swept down into tori's free left hand (b). Uke's hand is then swept up behind his back as tori applies downward pressure with his palm to the back of uke's head (c), causing the aggressor to flip head first over onto his back (d).

KAITEN-NAGE FACE-PUNCH DEFENSE
(CONTINUED)

CHAPTER

COMBINATION

DEFENSES

This chapter is designed to demonstrate the effectiveness of Aikido techniques against a variety of combination attacks used frequently by hard stylists. Dealing with the method of attack of another martial art is something that is rarely taught, not just in Aikido classes but in *any* martial art. Hard styles (Karate, Tang Soo Do, and Taekwondo, for example) very rarely teach you how to deal with people who trap and throw (Aikido, Jujitsu, Judo). Likewise, the softer styles seldom teach how to deal with the combination striking attacks of the hard stylists.

The only way to acquire a truly well-rounded martial-arts education that is applicable in any combat situation is to cross-train in this manner. During the feudal eras of both Europe and Asia, the warrior who was not well versed in the fighting styles of other systems was most often a dead warrior.

In the transition from military training to martial arts, this previously mandatory part of training has been lost in many systems. The difference between training in the dojo and training for the street, as I have said before, is in knowing what to expect from the other fighter. You must assume nothing regarding the other fighter's strategy or how much room you have to move, and you must be prepared for anything.

The assumption in many arts, as illustrated often in currently popular events such as the "Ultimate Fighting Challenge," is that your opponent will attack or respond in a certain way. When that does not happen, the defender is at a loss as to what to do and most often is defeated. In teaching seminars, I have heard the comment time and again from students and instructors that they are dismayed that their teachers never showed them how to deal with what other systems teach.

As you review the following sequences, you will see that they refer back to previous techniques. The reason they are separate here is the importance of the concept.

JAB/PUNCH DEFENSE

This sequence illustrates a defense against a combination of a left jab and a right cross. As uke attacks, tori parries the left jab with a rear-hand parry (a), followed by a lead-hand parry of the right cross. As the second parry is executed, tori simultaneously throws a rear cross to uke's chin, dazing him (b). This strike is then followed by ude-hishigi, which was detailed in chapter 8 (c).

TECHNIQUE TIPS—JAB/PUNCH DEFENSE

1. Deflect the initial jab with your rear hand, leaving your lead hand available to parry the next strike.
2. Counterstrike at the same time you parry the second strike.
3. You may apply any technique that starts with the lead-hand parry from this point.

FRONT-SNAP KICK/REVERSE-PUNCH DEFENSE

Defending against a combination front-snap kick and reverse punch, tori executes a leg-check block (a) to deflect the kick and then a lead-hand parry to the punching hand (b). He then follows up with a rear cross (c) and do-gaeshi, which was illustrated in chapter 9 (d).

TECHNIQUE TIPS—FRONT-SNAP KICK/
REVERSE-PUNCH DEFENSE

1. Maintain your balance while smothering your attacker's kick by not shifting your weight to the rear.
2. Keep your body upright, and do not reach for the attacking leg.
3. Parry uke's reverse punch with the lead hand, and counterstrike at the same time.

LOW ROUNDHOUSE KICK/BACKFIST DEFENSE

In this sequence, tori uses a leg check to stop an incoming low roundhouse kick (a) and uses a double-bone block against his opponent's backfist attack (b). He then counterstrikes with a vertical punch to uke's floating ribs (c) and executes kote-gaeshi, which was illustrated in chapter 7 (d).

TECHNIQUE TIPS—LOW ROUNDHOUSE KICK/ BACKFIST DEFENSE

1. Block the kick with the outside of your calf, not your knee.
2. Block uke's backfist with the back of your arm with a strong outward sweeping motion.
3. Use a vertical punch to uke's floating ribs, keeping your fist upright, not turned palm down.

CHAPTER

11

WEAPON
DEFENSES

he illustrations in this chapter will show you how to use the techniques you have learned thus far in defending against an armed opponent. Here, as with the other technical chapters, keep your finger in chapter 4 for quick reference.

Although these techniques are excellent for defending against the average person, you must always remember that someone who is an expert in handling a weapon will leave little opportunity for any defensive technique. By this I mean that a trained gunman will keep his distance from you and stay out of range of your grasp. The average person or hoodlum will prefer to get close to you and enjoy the terror when he sticks his gun in your face, ribs, or back.

Any situation involving a weapon should be avoided at all cost. Unless you are certain that the lack of any action on your part will result in the death of you or your loved ones, it is better to cooperate than to act. If you must act to save your life, the very best course of action, as shown here, is to take the weapon, as well as the arm holding it, totally out of commission and/or turn the weapon back on your attacker.

FRONT-GUN DEFENSE

Kote-gaeshi can be a highly effective technique to disarm your attacker when you are faced with a frontal threat from a gun. It is most important to remember that you must always maneuver to the outside of the gun hand. It is almost impossible to track a target to the outside of the body, and a quick pivot will put you out of the line of the muzzle.

KOTE-GAESHI FRONT-GUN DEFENSE

With the gun pointed at the stomach (a), tori makes a 90-degree pivot, shifting his right foot to the rear to remove himself from the line of fire while grasping the gun arm at the wrist at the same time (b). Tori immediately brings his right hand in and applies the palm of his hand to the back of uke's hand (c) and turns out into the kote-gaeshi wrist lock (d). Once the assailant is on the ground, tori directs the muzzle to uke's throat and slides his finger over uke's in the trigger guard, totally controlling the gun and the situation (e).

KOTE-GAESHI FRONT-GUN DEFENSE
(CONTINUED)

REAR-GUN DEFENSE

Kote-gaeshi is also an effective technique against a rear-gun attack. With the gun in your back, it is very important to pay attention to where the gun is making contact and from where the voice is coming. If the gunman is right-handed, he will place the gun just to the right of your spine, and his voice will come over your left shoulder. If he is left-handed, the gun will usually be just to the left of the spine, and his voice will come over your right shoulder. If the gun is held close to you but is not making contact, try to ascertain where your attacker is by the sound of his voice. This is of the utmost importance because you must guess correctly where the gun is in order to move to the outside of the weapon. Also, if he is too far away, your chances of controlling the gun are greatly reduced at best.

KOTE-GAESHI REAR-GUN DEFENSE

When faced with a rear-gun attack (a), tori pivots 360 degrees to the outside of the gun arm, striking it with his forearm on the way around to drive the gun away from his body (b). After completing the pivot, tori grabs the gun wrist with his left hand and controls it (c). Tori brings his right hand in and applies the palm of his hand to the back of uke's hand (d) and turns out into the kote-gaeshi wrist lock (e). Tori directs the muzzle to uke's throat and slides his finger over uke's in the trigger guard, totally controlling the gun and the situation (f) and takes uke to the ground (g).

TECHNIQUE TIPS—GUN DEFENSE

1. Do not try to take a gun if it is not within reach.
2. Do not try to fight a gunman unless you are sure you will die otherwise.
3. Always pivot to the outside of the gun hand, never across uke's body.

Kote-Gaeshi Rear-Gun Defense
(CONTINUED)

KOTE-GAESHI REAR-GUN DEFENSE
(CONTINUED)

KNIFE DEFENSES

A person trained as a knife expert, which is rare, will hold the blade so it points at your eyes, thus obscuring the position of the blade. An expert will seldom attempt to stab you, preferring to slash from side to side. In any knife situation, resign yourself to the fact that win or lose, you will most likely be cut at some point during the confrontation. The average person will attack in one of the ways illustrated here.

TECHNIQUE TIPS—KNIFE DEFENSE

1. Avoid a knife confrontation if at all possible.
2. Always back away from the knife.
3. If possible, use a technique that will break the arm holding the knife.
4. Try to keep the back of your forearm, where there are fewer nerves and blood vessels, toward the knife blade.

KNIFE LUNGE

A knife lunge is a straight-in attack, usually by an untrained fighter trying to stab you in the midsection. This can be much more dangerous than a slashing attack in that the attacker is coming straight in very rapidly. In this type of attack, it is clear that simply cutting you is not what this person has in mind; therefore, a much more damaging technique is called for in response. You must not only evade and control the attacker but also disarm or incapacitate him as well.

YUKI-CHIGAI KNIFE-LUNGE DEFENSE

In response to a knife lunge, tori steps back with his right foot, thus removing his abdomen as a target, and executes an arm-breaking block by slapping the inside of the wrist and outside of the elbow at the same time (a). Tori slides his left hand down to achieve the yuki-chigai backhand grip (b). Tori steps in under the arm, leading with his right foot (c) and bringing his left into line beside uke to complete the 180-degree pivot (d). Tori finishes this technique by bringing the knife blade in against the ribs, applying pressure to the outside of the hand to control the attacker (e).

YUKI-CHIGAI KNIFE-LUNGE DEFENSE
(CONTINUED)

ROBUSE KNIFE-LUNGE DEFENSE

As the knife comes in, tori steps to the rear and executes an **X**-block with the right hand on top (a). Tori grabs the wrist with his right hand (b) and draws it up and to the rear, bringing the back of the hand to rest on his knee (c). Because tori has not yet applied any force to make the attacker drop the knife, he delivers a downward strike with the fist or palm to the back of the elbow, breaking the arm and disarming his opponent (d).

ROBUSE KNIFE-LUNGE DEFENSE
(CONTINUED)

OVERHEAD STAB

An overhead stab is another tactic used by an untrained fighter. It is a technique designed to kill rather than cut. The attacker is coming down with all his strength to try to penetrate your rib cage. Here again, because this attack is designed to kill, use whatever amount of force is necessary to disarm your assailant.

UDE-GARAMI OVERHEAD-STAB DEFENSE

This is a new technique that translates as "entangled arm lock." This is only effective against the downward stabbing motion of an unskilled knife fighter. It is imperative that tori intercept the arm in motion while it is still bent and not let it become extended. If tori is too slow on this defense, the knife blade can easily be drawn down against him, cutting both arms severely.

As the knife arm begins to move, tori steps into the attack with his left foot and uses a modified X-block to stop the arm in motion (a). The block used here must be strong enough to stop the arm, so tori wants to catch the arm with his right hand, backing it up with the left hand locked onto his own wrist. As tori stops the motion, he brings his right knee up to strike the groin or the midsection (b). With the enemy now dazed, tori brings his left hand around uke's arm and feeds it through the space between his arm and uke's, exerting pressure against tori's own wrist with the outer edge of his hand (c). Tori applies pressure to the rear and downward, throwing the attacker to the rear (d).

UDE-GARAMI OVERHEAD-STAB DEFENSE
(CONTINUED)

CHAPTER

12

AIKIDO FITNESS

lthough Aikido is geared toward nonresistance, and use of physical strength has an adverse effect on the performance of the techniques, it is always desirable in any physical activity to strive for a certain level of fitness.

The purpose of physical conditioning in this art is not to develop brute strength but rather to prevent the injuries that can and do occur when the body is not used to the type of actions that are now in demand. To withstand the demands of Aikido, your body requires at least a minimal level of fitness and flexibility. The exercises shown in chapter 5 should help you acquire the flexibility needed in your joints to prevent injury. What we will discuss in this chapter are some strengthening exercises to build stronger muscles and connective tissues and provide endurance.

STRENGTH TRAINING

One of the most important considerations when using weights in conjunction with Aikido training is to maintain your flexibility. The heavier the weight used, the larger the muscle itself will become. It is therefore preferable to use a moderate amount of weight for each exercise and build increased strength and muscle tone.

Another consideration is how many sets and repetitions of each exercise to perform. Many theories exist on this subject, but the general rule of thumb I use to achieve maximum results is to do three sets of 10 to 15 repetitions for each exercise every other day. Your muscles require 48 hours to recuperate after a heavy workout, so never train the same muscle group daily.

I prefer to alternate my weight training of muscle groups rather than try to work all of them every other day. I work biceps, shoulders, and abdominals one day, then triceps, back, and chest the next. Lower-body exercise should also be done every other day whenever you prefer.

The last thing to consider when starting a weight-training program is how much weight to use to start out. I can tell you from years of experience that whatever weight you think you should use at the beginning will result in extremely sore muscles, possible injury, and delayed progress. Remember that an injury at the gym also means *delays in the dojo!*

Like most people, I always (until I finally learned better) had an inflated concept of my physical capabilities. I would start trying to lift what I did a year ago when I quit. Now I have learned to start lifting at exactly half of what I had previously used. A good practice is to start so low that you would be embarrassed for anyone to find out about it. If you start out very low and work up gradually over a few weeks, you will experience weight training without pain!

CHEST

Training of the chest is important in martial arts because it helps in throwing a strong punch and in any pushing activity by supplementing the arm's strength. This is most important should you end up on the ground and have to wrestle with an opponent.

BENCH PRESS

The bench press is designed to work the outer portion of the pectoral muscles of the chest, as well as the frontal head of the deltoid (the front shoulder where it connects to the chest). An additional benefit is to the medial (middle) head of the triceps.

Lie flat on a weight bench with your feet on the floor and your hips and head flat on the bench. Lift the barbell from the uprights and position it over your chest, arms fully extended but not locked. Slowly lower the bar to your chest, then press straight up to full extension.

Your grip must be at least shoulder-width on the bar. The wider the grip, the more the concentration on the outer portion of the pectoral muscles of the chest. Moving the grip closer works the inner part of the muscles. Remember to perform this exercise only if you have a capable spotter to assist you.

FLYS

Flys are performed while supine on a bench with two dumbbells. This exercise works the inner pectorals and deltoids.

The arms must be bent at the elbows at approximately a 45-degree angle and held firmly in place throughout the motion. Starting at the top with the weights up, lower them slowly out away from the body until the dumbbells are lower than chest level, then bring them back up to the starting position. Remember to keep your arms locked at a 45-degree angle and keep the elbows out to the sides away from the body.

SHOULDERS

The deltoid muscles of the shoulder girdle are three-headed muscles. The frontal head is strengthened by the bench press, so I'll concentrate here on the other two heads. Imbalanced shoulder development can lead to injury because one head outworks the capacity of the others, which can actually lead to dislocation during a heavy workout. Shoulder strength is essential in Aikido because of the pressure placed on the shoulder joint by locks.

UPRIGHT BARBELL ROWS

This exercise, which works the lateral deltoid, can be done with a barbell or two dumbbells. Using a grip that is less than shoulder-width and keeping the elbows higher than the bar, raise the bar up to the chin and then lower again.

BENT-OVER DUMBBELL ROWS

This exercise will strengthen your shoulders only if done correctly. Bend over at the waist and let the weight of the dumbbells or barbell hang straight down. Make sure that the shoulders do not hang but are held up in their natural position so the back is flat and parallel to the floor. Pull the weight up smoothly to your chest, then lower it to the starting position. When raising the

weight, keep the arms in close to the body and concentrate on raising the elbows without raising the shoulders. The easiest way to move the weight from this position is *not* the right way. If you pull up with the shoulders you will use the muscles of the back, not the shoulders.

BICEPS

Biceps are on the inside of the upper arm and are responsible for drawing the lower arm upward and lifting with the arm. Biceps also help to support the triceps when extending the arm by providing opposing muscle stability. Strong biceps will always be useful in escaping from an attacker's grasp.

BARBELL CURLS

Barbell curls build strength in the biceps. Standing erect, hold the barbell at arm's length, palms facing away from your body. In a slow and steady motion, raise the bar from the starting position until it is at chin level, then slowly lower it again. To get the maximum effect from this move, keep the elbows tucked in close to the body throughout the motion. Letting the elbows come out to the side will result in using muscles of the shoulder and back rather than the biceps to raise the bar.

DUMBBELL CURLS

When executing the dumbbell curl motion, start with the thumb pointed up, and, as you raise the weights, turn the thumb to the outside until the dumbbell is parallel to the floor. This extra turn of the wrist during each repetition will give not only strength but also thickness to the biceps. A side benefit is added strength and fullness to the forearm, which plays a major part in turning the weight.

TRICEPS

The triceps are the muscles on the outside of the upper arm that are used to straighten the arm. Strong triceps will add stability to certain techniques and help prevent injuries when you are on the receiving end of an armbar.

STANDING TRICEPS EXTENSIONS

You should use a cambered curling bar, a specially designed triceps bar, or two dumbbells held together. Starting with the weight held overhead and using a slow steady motion, lower the weight until it touches the back of the shoulders, and then press back up. The elbows must be held close to the sides of the head throughout the motion. Do not let the elbows fly out to the side or you will be using the chest and shoulder muscles to do the work, not the triceps.

LYING TRICEPS EXTENSIONS

Lie on your back on a bench with a dumbbell held overhead. Your palm should face downward toward your feet. Supporting the upper arm with your free hand, lower the weight across your chest until the dumbbell touches your shoulder, then raise it back to the starting position.

ABDOMINALS

Training of the abs can be both tedious and painful, but strong abs will prevent back problems. My favorite abdominal exercise is listed in the next section on "Cardio-Exercise Machines." It is no-impact training and puts no strain on either the back or the neck. The crunches described here will also work the upper and lower abdominal muscles.

CRUNCHES

Lie on your back with your pelvis tilted upward and the small of the back pressed down against the floor. Draw your feet toward the buttocks so the knees are at a 135-degree angle to the hips, keeping the feet together. Cross the arms over the chest and, tightening the abs, slowly raise the shoulders off the floor. Start with 10 repetitions, and increase slowly.

REVERSE CRUNCHES

Lie on your back with your hands under your buttocks and back firmly against the floor. Raise the knees toward the ceiling with the calves parallel to the floor. From this position, contract the abs, pulling the knees toward the chest; then return to the original position. Begin with 10 repetitions, and increase slowly.

BACK

The resistance exercises I outlined in the earlier section have a secondary effect of helping to build a strong upper back, but we need to concentrate some on the lower back, which is where most injuries occur. Abdominal training will have a very good effect on strengthening the lower back and giving your entire midsection good support, but it is usually not enough. Most people injure their lower backs by improper lifting and bending. Therefore, improving the muscle tone in this area will help to prevent this type of injury.

TOE TOUCHES

The easiest and most practical way to work the lower back is simply by keeping the feet together, bending forward slowly and smoothly to touch your toes, and standing back upright. This does not seem like much, but consider that most of your body weight is from your hips up, and you will realize how much your back is lifting each time you stand back up to a fully erect position. This exercise is especially good for those who have a weak back to begin with because it puts the least amount of strain on it (you can perform this exercise with your hands on your hips or thighs to further reduce back strain). Remember to perform this exercise smoothly with no bouncing and keep your knees slightly bent to avoid hyperextending the knees.

BENT-KNEE DEADLIFTS

Begin in a standing position with your feet shoulder-width apart and a dumbbell in each hand. While keeping your head up and your back straight, bend your knees until your hands are slightly below your knees, then use your legs and lower back to stand. As you stand up, keep the weight in front of your body. Once fully erect, pull the shoulders back, tuck your fanny in tightly, and then repeat. Start with very light dumbbells and 10 repetitions, and gradually work up to using a barbell. Remember, do not jerk or bounce in this motion. Perform each repetition slowly and deliberately using mostly leg strength to raise the weight.

LEGS

Walking is an excellent exercise for improving the strength of your legs, as well as a great cardiovascular exercise. All the exercises listed in the next section will improve muscle tone and stamina, as will walking, aerobics, martial-arts classes, stair-climbing machines, jumping rope, and swimming. The important thing is having legs that are strong and durable. Any exercise you do will help because your legs are already carrying your entire body weight as soon as you stand up.

CARDIOVASCULAR TRAINING

Training in Aikido will be whatever you put into it. If you want to go at a slow pace, then you will hardly ever break a sweat. If you practice hard and at a good pace, you will get a good endurance workout as well. Every good conditioning workout needs some aerobic activity as well as strength conditioning.

Running is a very good aerobic exercise but can be hard on the knees and ankles. Martial-arts training of any kind can be hard enough on the knees and ankles over the long run, without adding extra stress to these joints. For this reason I prefer these exercises.

TRAMPOLINE

Running in place on a trampoline gives the same aerobic effect without stressing the knee joints. The impact is almost completely absorbed by the springs on the trampoline, so you get all the benefits of running without any of the potential for injury. Set up your running pace and maintain for at least 15 to 20 minutes. You should start out at about five to seven minutes and work up.

CARDIO-EXERCISE MACHINES

These machines are rather new, but they offer an excellent nonimpact aerobic workout while the exerciser is seated. Many are advertised on television and are available from most of the major department stores, running from $150 to $250. It is recommended that you use these machines three times a week for 20 minutes a session. They have adjustable tension to provide a good muscle or aerobic workout.

By altering your grip and foot positions, you can shift emphasis from a full-body aerobic activity to a good midsection workout that works the lower back and the abdominals.

Cardio-exercise machine.

OTHER ACTIVITIES

As I mentioned earlier, any activity that gets you on your feet and in motion for an extended time provides a cardiovascular benefit and increases endurance. Get out there and dance, hike, bike, ski, walk, swim, jump rope, or take aerobics or martial-arts classes. Do whatever you like to do, but just get moving and keep in motion for at least 20 minutes three times a week.

You can do hundreds of possible exercises to strengthen your body and improve your cardiovascular fitness, and I could spend many chapters on each body part. Because this is a martial-arts book rather than a fitness manual, I have only included those that are my favorites and that I have found to be effective for my own personal training. As you begin setting up your own fitness program, consult other books written specifically about strength and cardiovascular training for other ideas and consult your physician if you have specific health concerns.

SUGGESTED READINGS

Bennett, G. 1992. *Intro to Tejitsu-ryu.* Derry, Pennsylvania: Tejitsu-ryu International.

———. 1994. *Tejitsu-ryu grappling techniques.* Derry, Pennsylvania: Tejitsu-ryu International.

Corcoran, J., and E. Farkas. 1988. *Martial arts traditions, history, people.* New York: W.H. Smith.

Le, V. 1977. *Course syllabus for Yoseikan Aikido.*

Lowry, D. 1981. O'Sensei: Aikido's Uyeshiba. *Black Belt* 19:28-33 and 82-83.

Nitobe, I. 1899. *Bushido, the soul of Japan* (reprint, Santa Clarita, CA: Ohara Publications, 1979).

Pruim, A. 1990. A karate compendium. *Black Belt* 28:18-22.

Shioda, G. 1968. *Dynamic aikido.* Japan: Kodansha International.

Thomas, S. 1974. Richard Bowe: Master of Aikido. *Masters of Self Defense* 1:8-9.

Westbrook, A., and O. Ratti. 1970. *Aikido and the dynamic sphere.* Tokyo: Charles E. Tuttle Co.

Yamada, S., and A. Macintosh. 1966. *The principles and practice of Aikido.* New York: Arco.

INDEX

groin kick
    basic technique 77
    with circular breakout 86
    with lift 87
gun defenses 150-157
Gung-fu (Kung-fu) 4, 14, 34
gyaku-ate 138
gyaku-katate-tori. *See* grip #2

H

hakama 8, 27-28
hana-nage 138
hando-no-kuzushi 40
happo-no-kuzushi 40
harmonious approach, in Aikido 1,
    20-21
Hirai, Minoru 21, 24
history, of Aikido 13-15, 19-21
Hombu Aikido vi, 22
honesty, as samurai value 18-19
honor, as samurai value 19
Hoshi, Tetsumis 23
Hwarang-do 14

I

IAF (International Aikido
        Federation) 22
Inoue, Yoichiro 23
instruction
    choice of instructor 3, 5-6
    choice of martial art for study 3-5
    choice of school 3, 6-8
    cost and pricing of 7-8
instructors
    how to choose 3, 5-6
    proper form of address 26-27
integrity, as samurai value 17
International Aikido Federation
        (IAF) 22

J

jab/punch defense 142-143
Judo 4, 22, 34, 141
Jujitsu 41, 141
    basic principles 34
    as basis for Aikido 1
    Gracie Jujitsu 53
    history of 14-15, 19, 20
justifiable force 4, 44-45

K

kaiten-nage 139-140
Kano, Jigoro 22
Karate vii, 3, 34, 41, 141

katate-tori. *See* grip #1
Keijutsukai Aikido 24
Kenjutsu 15, 20
kicks 3-4. *See also* groin kick
    defenses for
        blocks 70, 72
        for front-snap kick/reverse-
            punch 144-145
        for low roundhouse kick/
            backfist 146-147
ki (power) principle 37-39
Kito-ryu Jujitsu 15
knife defenses 157-166
Kobu-jutsu Aikido 23
Korindo Aikido 21, 24
kote-gaeshi
    basic guidelines 90-91
    body-punch defense 92-93
    face-punch defense 37, 47-50
    grip #6 defense 94-95
    gun defenses 150-157
kote-kudaki 106-110
    basic guidelines 106
    body-punch defense 109-110
    grip #3 defense 107-108
kubi-waza 133
Kung-fu (Gung-fu) 4, 14, 34
kyu ranks 8-9

L

language (terms) 25-34
lead-hand parry 68
lead punch
    defenses for
        do-gaeshi 136-137
        mukae-daoshi 128-129
    self-defense technique 73-74
Lee, Bruce 39
legal force 4, 44-45
leg check 72
lift and groin kick 87
line (sen) principle 39-40
low roundhouse kick/backfist
        defense 146-147
loyalty, as samurai value 19

M

mae-ryote-tori. *See* grip #5
Makiyama, Thomas 24
manners
Aikido principles for 26-27, 28
of samurai 18
martial arts. *See also specific arts*
    cross-training for dealing with
        other styles 141-142

ABOUT THE
AUTHOR

Gary Bennett is ranked as a 10th-degree black belt (Judan) and Soke (Grandmaster) of Tejitsu Aikido, the system he founded in 1989. His memberships have included the New World Martial Arts Association, the Eastern U.S.A. International Martial Arts Association (EUSAIMAA), the Bushido-Brotherhood Martial Arts Society, and the World Head of Family Sokeship Council (WHFSC). Grandmaster Bennett is a five-time Martial Arts Hall of Fame inductee. He currently serves on the Executive Advisory Council of EUSAIMAA and is a WHFSC membership screener for the northeast quadrant of the United States.

Bennett's dojo is located in Latrobe, Pennsylvania, where he trains a select group of dedicated students. He is an Aikido instructor for Westmoreland County Community College, a seminar instructor and promoter, and a volunteer who teaches self-defense to abuse victims and provides training for youth home employees. Bennett has authored a number of instructional books and articles and has produced training videos for Tejitsu Aikido.

Gary Bennett lives in Derry, Pennsylvania, with his wife, Debra Ann. They enjoy walking and bicycling. You are invited to visit his website at www.tejitsu.com.

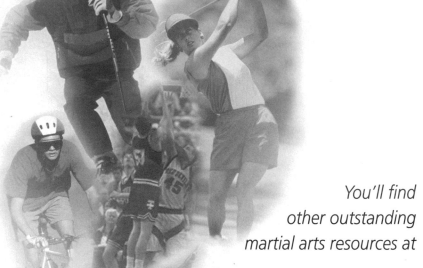

*You'll find
other outstanding
martial arts resources at*

www.humankinetics.com

In the U.S. call

1-800-747-4457

Australia	08 82771555
Canada.................................	800-465-7301
Europe	+44 (0) 113 278 1708
New Zealand	09-309-1890